GREATER MEKONG SUBREGION GENDER STRATEGY IMPLEMENTATION PLAN 2025–2030

SEPTEMBER 2024

ADB

CONTENTS

TABLES AND FIGURES   v

ACKNOWLEDGMENTS   vi

ABBREVIATIONS   vii

EXECUTIVE SUMMARY   viii

1   INTRODUCTION

Background: Integration of Gender Equality into the GMS	1
Gender Equality Elements of the GMS Program Before the GMS Program	
Strategic Framework 2030	2
Gender Equality Elements of the GMS Program Strategic Framework 2030	4
Purpose of the Gender Strategy Implementation Plan (2025–2030)	5

2   OVERVIEW OF THE GENDER STRATEGY

Assessment of Gender Issues	9
Objectives	10
Gender Mainstreaming Entry Points	11
Implementation Mechanisms	13
Results Framework	14

3   THE GENDER STRATEGY IMPLEMENTATION PLAN 2025–2030

Management Systems for Delivering the Implementation Plan	18
Gender Strategy Objective 1	19
Gender Elements of the Sectors' Strategic Frameworks and Action Plans	20
Gender Elements of the GMS Regional Investment Framework Projects	21
Guidance Note for Mainstreaming Gender in GMS	23
Regional Investment Framework Projects	
Gender Strategy Objective 2	25
Gender Strategy Objective 3	26

4 RESULTS FRAMEWORK

Level 1. Regional Development Context: Impacts   33
Level 2. Sector and Subsector Outcomes and Outputs   33
Level 3. Institutional Effectiveness   35

5 ESTIMATED COST OF FINANCING AND WAY FORWARD

36

APPENDIXES

1   Greater Mekong Subregion Program Institutional Structure   39
        and the Roles of its Different Levels in Implementing the
        Greater Mekong Subregion Program Gender Strategy
2   Greater Mekong Subregion Gender Strategy's   42
        Crosscutting Themes and Examples of Actions Per Theme
3   Greater Mekong Subregion Gender Strategy   43
        Implementation Plan Gantt Chart of Activities
4   Assessment of the Gender Elements of the   44
        Greater Mekong Subregion Sectors' Strategic Frameworks

TABLES AND FIGURES

TABLES

1 Gender Mainstreaming in Recent Strategic Frameworks   20
   of Eight Greater Mekong Subregion Sectors

2 Setting Up the Management Systems for Delivering the   26
   Greater Mekong Subregion Gender Strategy Implementation Plan

3 Implementation Plan for Developing the Capacity of the   27
   Greater Mekong Subregion Program to Achieve the
   Gender Strategy Objective 1

4 Implementation Plan for Developing the Capacity of the   29
   Greater Mekong Subregion Program to Achieve the
   Gender Strategy Objective 2

5 Implementation Plan for Developing the Capacity of the   31
   Greater Mekong Subregion Program to Achieve the
   Gender Strategy Objective 3

6 Estimated Cost of the Greater Mekong Subregion   37
   Gender Strategy Implementation Plan 2025–2030 (tentative)

FIGURES

1 Pillars and Priority Sectors of the Greater Mekong Subregion Program   2

2 The Greater Mekong Subregion Program Institutional Structure   6

3 Objectives of the Greater Mekong Subregion Gender Strategy   11

4 Implementation Mechanisms of the Greater Mekong Subregion   14
   Gender Strategy

5 Greater Mekong Subregion Program Gender Strategy   17
   Implementation Plan: Theory of Change

ACKNOWLEDGMENTS

The Greater Mekong Subregion (GMS) Gender Strategy Implementation Plan was prepared by Brenda Batistiana, consultant, with invaluable inputs and feedback from the Ministry of Labor, Invalids, and Social Affairs (Viet Nam); Lao Women's Union (Lao People's Democratic Republic [Lao PDR]); All China Women's Federation (People's Republic of China [PRC]); the Department of Women Affairs and Family Institutions, Ministry of Social Development and Human Security (Thailand); and the Ministry of Women's Affairs (Cambodia). Acknowledging also the support and insights provided by GMS national secretariats and other GMS ministries that participated in the consultative process. The inputs and support from the Asian Development Bank (ADB) Gender Equality Division, especially Chieko Yokota (gender specialist), and from the Human and Social Development Group with Francesco Tornieri (principal social development specialist–Social Inclusion), are gratefully acknowledged. Valuable inputs were likewise provided by Veronica Mendizabal Joffre (senior gender and social development specialist, ADB) and the gender officers in ADB's resident missions, namely, Fei Huang (gender officer, PRC), Theonakhet Saphakdy (senior social development officer–Gender, Lao People's Democratic Republic), Chandy Chea (senior social development officer–Gender, Cambodia) and Giang Thanh Nguyen (senior social development officer–Gender, Viet Nam). Finally, the GMS Secretariat with the special support and guidance from Asadullah Sumbal (principal regional cooperation specialist, GMS Secretariat, ADB), Alfredo Perdiguero (unit head, Regional Cooperation and Integration, Southeast Asia Department, ADB), Lucia Martin Casanueva (consultant, GMS Secretariat, ADB), Josephine Duque-Comia (senior programs officer, GMS Secretariat, ADB), and Cira Rudas (senior operations assistant, GMS Secretariat, ADB).

ABBREVIATIONS

ADB	Asian Development Bank
GMS	Greater Mekong Subregion
GMS-2030	Greater Mekong Subregion Economic Cooperation Program Strategic Framework 2030
GSIP	Gender Strategy Implementation Plan
MTR	midterm review
RIF	Regional Investment Framework
SDG	Sustainable Development Goal
SOGIE	sexual orientations and gender identities and expressions
SOGIESC	sexual orientations, gender identities and expressions, and sex characteristics

EXECUTIVE SUMMARY

One core agenda of the Greater Mekong Subregion Economic Cooperation Program (GMS Program) Strategic Framework 2030 (GMS-2030) is promoting gender equality. Regional cooperation involves countries comprising the GMS (i.e., Cambodia, the People's Republic of China, the Lao People's Democratic Republic, Myanmar, Thailand, and Viet Nam). The GMS-2030 also gears the regional cooperation initiatives toward helping the individual countries deliver their United Nations Sustainable Development Goal (SDG) commitments, including SDG 5 (achieve gender equality and empower all women and girls) and SDG 10 (reduce inequality within and among countries). This aim is upheld in the GMS-2030's principle of inclusivity, which means ensuring lower-income populations, including women, benefit from the GMS Program's initiatives along its three pillars (i.e., community, connectivity, and competitiveness).

The GMS-2030 gender equality agenda is elaborated in its Gender Strategy, which was endorsed by the ministers and heads of delegations from the governments of the GMS countries on 8 December 2022 during the 25th Ministerial Meeting of the GMS Program and published in the same month. A Gender Strategy Implementation Plan (GSIP) 2025–2030 was developed in consultation with the GMS national secretariats, including the gender focal persons of each GMS country. The GSIP was approved during the GMS Senior Officials Meeting on 17 May 2024.

The GSIP provides four sets of activities, target outputs, and performance indicators to develop the capacity of the GMS Program or set up the basic requirements to achieve the Gender Strategy's three objectives, which are written in the Gender Strategy paper as follows:

(i) Improve existing methods and develop new and innovative approaches to gender mainstreaming to ensure equal access and participation in opportunities arising from the GMS Program;
(ii) Complement subregional efforts to explicitly address gender barriers affecting the full participation of individuals of all ages, abilities, and in all socioeconomic spheres; and
(iii) Address pervasive gender norms that disadvantage one group over another.

The GSIP's four sets of activities are the following:

(i) Activities aimed to establish the management systems, including forming a Task Force on Gender, for delivering the GSIP. The Task Force on Gender will comprise two representatives (gender focal persons) from each GMS country and will be assisted by the GMS Secretariat, based in the Regional Cooperation Division of the Asian Development Bank Southeast Asia Department. The country representatives to the task force will ensure that the delivery of the GSIP aligns with ongoing national gender strategies and plans.

(ii) Activities aimed to strengthen the integration of gender equality principles and approaches in the GMS Program's core operations, which are its eight sectors and the single-country and multi-country projects under its Regional Investment Framework. A guidance note or common guidelines will be developed for mainstreaming gender in gender-relevant Regional Investment Framework projects.

(iii) Activities aimed to build the GMS Program's knowledge base in promoting gender equality through an intersectionality lens (looking at how gender inequality intersects with other sources of discrimination and vulnerabilities, such as age, ability or disability, and sexual orientation and gender identity) and establish the GMS Program as an emerging knowledge resource in mainstreaming gender in regional cooperation initiatives.

(iv) More activities to expand the knowledge base on gender mainstreaming approaches through pilot projects and gender forums on emerging gender-related issues and initiatives to be conducted every 3 years.

In line with the Gender Strategy's proposition, the GSIP proposes integrating gender performance indicators into the GMS-2030 Results Framework instead of having a separate gender-specific evaluation document. The GSIP offers gender performance indicators at the three levels (impacts, sector and subsector outcomes and outputs, and institutional effectiveness) of the results framework for consideration during its midterm review.

Women in the handicrafts industry. Weaving is a traditional handicraft of the Ta Oi, an ethnic group in Viet Nam. Many women preserve and develop the traditional cloth weaving and introduce it to tourists through the support of ADB's Greater Mekong Subregion Sustainable Tourism Development Project.

1

INTRODUCTION

This Gender Strategy Implementation Plan (GSIP) 2025–2030 aims to operationalize the Gender Strategy of the Greater Mekong Subregion (GMS) Strategic Framework 2030 (GMS-2030).[1] The Gender Strategy, which elaborates on the core gender equality agenda of GMS-2030, was endorsed by the ministers and heads of delegations from the governments of the GMS countries on 8 December 2022 during the 25th Ministerial Meeting of the GMS Program

BACKGROUND: INTEGRATION OF GENDER EQUALITY INTO THE GMS

The GMS comprises Cambodia, the People's Republic of China (PRC, specifically Yunnan Province and Guangxi Zhuang Autonomous Region), the Lao People's Democratic Republic (Lao PDR), Myanmar, Thailand, and Viet Nam. In 1992, these six countries, with the assistance of the Asian Development Bank (ADB), launched the GMS Economic Cooperation Program to support high-priority subregional projects in various sectors, including agriculture, energy, environment, health, tourism, transport, trade facilitation, and urban development. The GMS Program began as an activity-based regional endeavor focused on sector-specific

Six GMS countries launched the GMS Economic Cooperation Program in 1992 to boost their economic cooperation.

Their vision is an "integrated and prosperous GMS through enabling policy environment, infrastructure linkages, and human resource and skills development."

initiatives.[2] Then, in 2001, the program—as stipulated in its first 10-year Strategic Framework covering 2002–2012[3]—adopted a holistic vision of "integrated and prosperous GMS to be achieved through an enabling policy environment and infrastructure linkages, as well as the development of human resources and skills."[4] Subsequently, in 2005, the GMS government leaders declared "connectivity, competitiveness, and community" as key pillars for achieving the GMS vision,[5] adopting the objective of the regional cooperation strategy and program, which ADB developed in 2004

The GMS Program's strategy to achieve the vision is along three pillars: connectivity, competitiveness, and community.

---

[1] ADB. 2022. *Greater Mekong Subregion Gender Strategy*.
[2] ADB. 2008. *Greater Mekong Subregion Maturing and Moving Forward: Evaluation Study*.
[3] ADB. 2002. *Building on Success: A Strategic Framework for the Next Ten Years of the Greater Mekong Subregion Economic Cooperation Program*.
[4] Footnote 2, p. 4, para. 11. The document lists five features of the first 10-year Strategic Framework that made it different from the earlier GMS program: (i) a more multisectoral approach to regional cooperation with a focus on developing the same geographic space as economic corridors; (ii) formal integration of the GMS priority projects into the six countries' national development plans; (iii) addition of subregional agriculture development to address price control and the role of infrastructure in reducing the cost of selling agricultural products; (iv) active engagement of the private sector as financier and development partner being the main engine of growth for the GMS; and (v) development of a comprehensive development matrix to plan and program, built around 11 flagship programs and with government commitment to assure priority financing of the national components of these programs.
[5] ADB. 2011. *The Greater Mekong Subregion Economic Cooperation Program Strategic Framework 2012–2022*. p. 3.

Figure 1. Pillars and Priority Sectors of the Greater Mekong Subregion Program

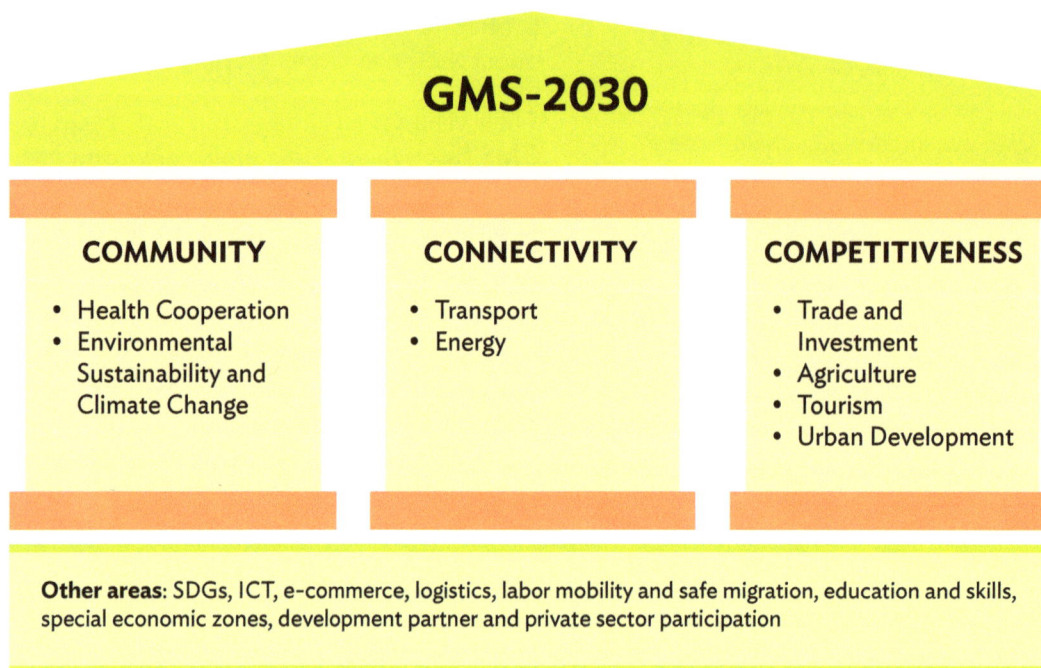

GMS-2030

COMMUNITY

- Health Cooperation
- Environmental Sustainability and Climate Change

CONNECTIVITY

- Transport
- Energy

COMPETITIVENESS

- Trade and Investment
- Agriculture
- Tourism
- Urban Development

Other areas: SDGs, ICT, e-commerce, logistics, labor mobility and safe migration, education and skills, special economic zones, development partner and private sector participation

GMS-2030 = Greater Mekong Subregion Economic Cooperation Program Strategic Framework 2030, ICT = information and communication technology, SDG = Sustainable Development Goal.
Source: ADB. 2022. *Greater Mekong Subregion Gender Strategy*. p. 7.

to support the GMS strategic framework.[6] The GMS Program's priority sectors are distributed into these three pillars (Figure 1).

In line with these pillars, the GMS Program defined its three strategies:[7]

(i) Increase physical infrastructure and transform transport corridors into transnational economic corridors through sustainable development;

(ii) Improve cross-border movement of people and goods and integrating markets, production processes, and value chains through efficient facilitation; and

(iii) Build a greater sense community of through projects and programs that address shared social and environmental concerns.

Gender Equality Elements of the GMS Program Before the GMS Program Strategic Framework 2030

The GMS Program in 1992–2001 and its first 10-year Strategic Framework 2002–2012 included a few services for women, particularly

---

[6] Footnote 2, p. 4, para. 11. The objective of ADB's regional cooperation strategy and program for the GMS is poverty reduction, which is to be achieved through a vision of connectivity, competitiveness, and a greater sense of community (known as the three Cs).

[7] ADB. 2015. *Greater Mekong Subregion Economic Cooperation Program*. p. 1.

the prevention of trafficking, facilitating safe migration, and providing jobs. Specifically, in the GMS operations from 1992 to 2007, one project, Preventing the Trafficking of Women and Children and Promoting Safe Migration, explicitly catered to women's needs.[8] The 10-year GMS Strategic Framework 2002–2012 had some progress with the addition of the provision of jobs to women in the objectives of its two flagship programs: North–South Economic Corridor Program and East–West Economic Development.[9]

Across the GMS Program sectors, promoting gender equality was first mentioned in the GMS Tourism Sector Strategy 2006–2015, which aimed, among its other objectives, to "contribute to poverty reduction, gender equality, empowerment of women, and sustainable development."[10] The second GMS Program 10-year Strategic Framework (2012–2022)—covering all eight sectors (Figure 1)—retained this objective for the tourism sector, its only section explicitly mentioning gender equality as a thrust.[11] Its Program Results Framework 2012–2022 (in its Annex) mirrored this feature, with the tourism sector as the only sector with a gender-related sector output indicator. This indicator focused solely on women and not explicitly on gender equality, i.e., "improved tourism infrastructure (pro-poor, pro-women, and environmentally friendly)."

Another sector, i.e., human resources development, also had "improving the capacity of vulnerable groups, including women," among the areas of its action plan but had no support indicator in the Program Results Framework.[12] This sector was replaced by the health sector in 2017 with the restructuring of the Working Group on Human Resource

Promoting gender equality as a principle and objective was initiated in the GMS Program by the GMS tourism sector. Then, three other sectors followed suit: health cooperation (formerly human resource development), agriculture, and environment.

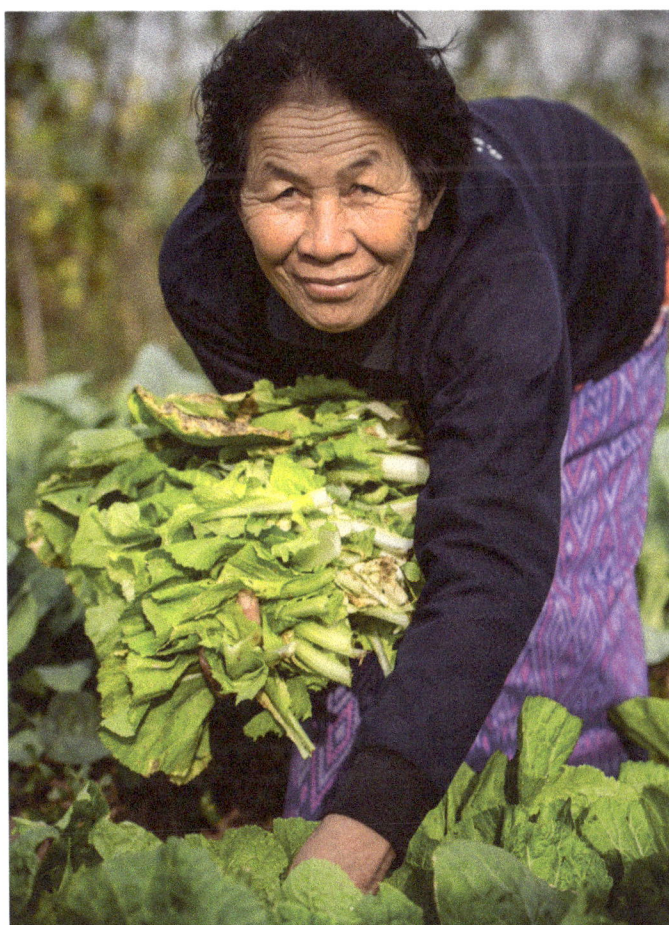

Women in agriculture. Woman working in an organic farm in Ban Mo, Thailand.

---

8 Footnote 2, Appendix 2, p. 64.
9 Footnote 3, Appendix 2, pp. 57–58.
10 ADB. 2011. *Greater Mekong Subregion Tourism Sector Assessment, Strategy, and Roadmap*.
11 Footnote 5, p. 16. However, this aim to "contribute to poverty reduction, gender equality, empowerment of women, and sustainable development" is not explicit in the GMS Tourism Sector Strategy 2016–2025.
12 Footnote 5, p. 18.

Development into the Working Group on Health Cooperation.[13] Gender mainstreaming is one of the three crosscutting themes of the GMS Health Cooperation Strategy 2019–2023 programmatic areas.[14]

While not mentioned in the second GMS Program 10 year Strategic Framework (2012–2022), the advancement of gender equality was prominently incorporated in two more sectors' strategic frameworks (agriculture and environment) for the same period. The Core Agriculture Support Program's Strategy

The advancement of gender equality in the GMS Program took a quantum leap forward in the GMS Program Strategic Framework 2030 (GMS-2030).

The GMS-2030 aims to gear regional cooperation toward helping the GMS countries deliver their SDG commitments, including SDG 5 and SDG 10.

for Promoting Safe and Environment-friendly Agro-based Value Chains in the GMS and Siem Reap Action Plan, 2018–2022 explicitly fostered gender equality in its overall purpose ("security of safe food for all, irrespective of a person's demographic, income status, and gender"), common guiding principles ("gender empowerment"), and design and monitoring framework (with gender-related performance indicators at the outcome level and two of

four outputs).[15] Similarly, the GMS Core Environment Program Strategic Framework and Action Plan 2018–2022 included in its list of guiding principles the adoption of an integrated value-chain approach to, among others, promote gender and social inclusiveness.[16] The Core Environment Program did not explicitly include promoting gender equality in its strategic approach, thematic areas, types of service intervention, and activities. Its gender feature was its intended indirect benefits to households ("gender-inclusive employment opportunities from more integrated value chains") and communities ("greater social and gender inclusion").

Gender Equality Elements of the GMS Program Strategic Framework 2030

Given its scant mention in the earlier GMS Program strategic frameworks, the advancement of gender equality can be described as taking a quantum leap forward in the GMS Program Strategic Framework 2030 (GMS-2030). This current framework aims to, among its other objectives, gear regional cooperation toward helping the individual countries deliver their United Nations Sustainable Development Goals (SDGs) commitments, including SDG 5 ("achieve gender equality and empower all women and girls") and SDG 10 ("reduce inequality within and among countries").[17] This aim is upheld in GMS-2030's principle of inclusivity, which means ensuring the benefit of lower-income populations, including women, from the GMS Program's future interventions and its three pillars (i.e., community, connectivity,

---

[13]   ADB. 2020. *Strategic Results Framework for the Greater Mekong Subregion Health Cooperation Strategy 2019–2023*.

[14]   ADB. 2019. *Greater Mekong Subregion Health Cooperation Strategy 2019–2023*.

[15]   ADB. 2018. *Strategy for Promoting Safe and Environment-Friendly Agro-based Value Chains in the GMS and Siem Reap Action Plan, 2018–2022*. pp. viii, 15, and 39–43. To apply the "gender empowerment" principle, the Siem Reap Action Plan states, "Policy development should address activities that will empower women and ensure equal benefit sharing between women and men. There is potential for empowering women and men smallholder farmers by introducing gender-sensitive agronomic practices that can strengthen their capacity in production, processing, and trade as well as improve gender equity in [the] agriculture sector with equal opportunity and benefit sharing for women and men."

[16]   GMS Environment Operations Center, ADB. 2017. *Greater Mekong Subregion Core Environment Program Strategic Framework and Action Plan 2018–2022*.

[17]   ADB. 2021. *The Greater Mekong Subregion Economic Cooperation Program Strategic Framework 2030*. p. 15.

and competitiveness). The GMS-2030 also "acknowledges the intersectional impacts of gender inequalities across all priority areas, as well as the need for specific and integrated approaches for advancing gender equality and the empowerment of women, girls, men, and boys across the subregion."[18] Elaborations on the GMS-2030's gender equality objectives are in its Gender Strategy (explained in section II), for which this implementation plan was developed.

PURPOSE OF THE GENDER STRATEGY IMPLEMENTATION PLAN (2025–2030)

The GSIP 2025–2030 purports to put into action the GMS-2030 Gender Strategy by providing specific activities, performance indicators, and systems or mechanisms to develop the capacity of the GMS Program to achieve the main objectives defined by the GMS Gender Strategy endorsed in 2022:[19]

(i) Improve existing methods and develop new and innovative approaches to gender mainstreaming to ensure equal access and participation in opportunities arising from the GMS Program;[20]

(ii) Complement subregional efforts to explicitly address gender barriers affecting the full participation of individuals of all ages, abilities, and in all socioeconomic spheres;[21] and

(iii) Address pervasive gender norms that disadvantage one group over another.

The gender equality agenda of the GMS-2030 is presented in a Gender Strategy paper, published in 2022.

The Gender Strategy has three objectives:

- **Improve the GMS Program's existing methods for gender mainstreaming.**
- **Complement subregional efforts to address gender barriers to participating in and benefiting from regional cooperation.**
- **Address pervasive gender norms.**

The GSIP provides the activities to develop the GMS Program's capacity to move toward achieving these three objectives.

In aiming to develop the capacity of the GMS Program, this GSIP lays the ground or sets up the basic requirements for achieving the three objectives.

The intended primary users of the GSIP are the various groups that comprise the GMS Program institutional structure, primarily the GMS Task Force on Gender (to be established as part of this implementation plan), GMS senior officials, GMS national secretariats, GMS sector working groups and task force, and GMS secretariat (Figure 2).[22] The GMS sector working groups are the (i) Subregional Transport Forum, Cross-Border Transport Agreement, National Transport Facilitation Committee, and GMS Railways Association for the transport sector; (ii) Energy Transition

---

[18] Footnote 17, p. 36, para. 128.

[19] Footnote 1, pp. vi–vii. These objectives were taken verbatim from the Gender Strategy paper.

[20] The identification and assessment of the GMS Program's existing methods for gender mainstreaming are part of this GSIP. These existing methods are linked with the GMS Program's two main strategies—thematic sectors and projects under the Regional Investment Framework (RIF)—and with the Gender Strategy's cross-cutting themes. The Gender Strategy considers these three methods as the GMS Program's gender mainstreaming entry points.

[21] The GMS Strategy has two formulations of its second objective. This implementation plan uses the formulation in the executive summary and not the one in Figure 1 on p. 5 as it explicitly addresses gender barriers.

[22] This implementation plan was completed in consultation with the gender and women ministries of the GMS countries and presented to national secretariats, sector working groups, and task forces for validation, and to the GMS senior officials during the Senior Officials' Meeting on 17 May 2024, where it was endorsed in principle.

Figure 2: The Greater Mekong Subregion Program Institutional Structure

Summit of Leaders
Broad strategic and long-term directions
Global trends affecting GMS
Progress on RCI
Triennial

Ministerial Conference
Policy direction on specific issues, themes, and institutional matters
Progress overview
Results-oriented initiatives
Annual

Development Partners
Development Partners' Meeting (DPM)

Senior Officials' Meetings
Policy setting
Operational matters

Sectoral Ministerial Meetings
On need basis

Thematic Forums

Sector Working Groups and Forums

Private Sector

GMS Secretariat
Technical, organizational, and coordination support

GMS Knowledge Network

Six GMS National Secretariats
Country knowledge and field support

Sectoral Ministerial Meetings

CBTA Joint Committee Meeting
Environment Ministers' Meeting
Agriculture Ministers' Meeting
Tourism Ministers' Meeting

Thematic Forums

1. Economic Corridors Forum – Annual
2. GMS Economic Corridor Governors' Forum – Annual; spearheaded by the PRC
3. GMS Business Forum/Council
4. Development Partners' Meeting
5. GMS Knowledge Network

Sector Working Groups and Forums

1. Subregional Transport Forum
2. CBTA National Transport Facilitation Committee
3. GMS Railways Association
4. Energy Transition Taskforce
5. Working Group on Environment
6. Working Group on Agriculture
7. Working Group on Tourism
8. Working Group on Health Cooperation
9. Working Group on Urban Development
10. Taskforce on Trade and Investment

In some cases, task forces are created for an interim period with the intention of formalizing these into working groups.

PRC = People's Republic of China, CBTA = Cross-Border Transport Agreement, GMS = Greater Mekong Subregion, RCI = Regional Cooperation and Integration.
Source: Asian Development Bank.

Taskforce (formerly Regional Power Trade Coordination Committee) for the energy sector; (iii) Working Group on Environment; (iv) Working Group on Agriculture; (v) Working Group on Tourism; (vi) Working Group on Health Cooperation; (vii) Working Group on Urban Development; and (viii) Task Force on Trade and Investment.[23] Appendix 1 describes their roles.

The GMS-2030 Gender Strategy is based on an assessment of the gender situation in the six GMS countries, conducted in 2021.

The Gender Strategy paper presents the results of the gender assessment and highlights five common barriers to gender equality in participation and benefit from regional cooperation.

---

[23] GMS Program. 2022. *Greater Mekong Subregion: Establishing the Task Force on Trade and Investment.*

2

OVERVIEW OF THE GENDER STRATEGY

Smallholder farmers development. A woman waters crops in Boung Phao Village, Lao People's Democratic Republic, as part of ADB's Sustainable Natural Resources and Productivity Enhancement Project.

ASSESSMENT OF GENDER ISSUES

The GMS Gender Strategy is based on the findings of an assessment of the status of gender equality in the six GMS countries.[24] Overall, the desk review of international and national data—e.g., the Gender Inequality Index of the United Nations Development Programme Human Development Reports[25] and the Social Institutions and Gender Index of the Organisation for Economic Co-operation and Development[26]—spanning 2010–2019 (2020 for some indicators) showed that "while all GMS countries have made progress toward gender equality, and many have adopted their national gender strategies, gender inequalities persist in the subregion."[27] Moreover, "although all GMS countries have adopted country-specific strategies to achieve Sustainable Development Goal 5 on gender equality, persistent issues with gender impacts remain."[28] This overall finding implies that women have not equally participated in and benefited from the GMS regional cooperation. According to the Gender Strategy, "a renewed effort is needed to prevent and manage these impacts and advance gender equality in the region."[29]

The GMS gender assessment highlighted five common barriers to women's equal participation and access to the benefits from GMS economic cooperation (footnote 29):

(i) social norms that assign individuals to specific gender roles;

Women and gender roles. A group of women harvesting flowers at a greenhouse in Viet Nam. The GMS gender assessment found that women in the subregion are still assigned specific gender roles.

---

[24] GMS Secretariat. GMS Gender Assessment. Unpublished. This assessment was finalized after the GMS Senior Officials Meeting on 10 March 2022.

[25] The Gender Inequality Index assesses the gender gap between women and men based on maternal mortality ratio, adolescent birth rate, women's share of seats in parliament, and the comparison of female and male populations with at least a secondary education and labor force participation rate.

[26] The Social Institutions and Gender Index measures discrimination against women through examining social norms, practices, and formal laws.

[27] Footnote 1, p. vi and p. 2.

[28] Footnote 1, p. 2 para. 9.

[29] Footnote 1, p. 6, para. 24.

The GMS Gender Strategy acknowledges the compounding effects of the intersection of gender inequality with other dimensions of discrimination and vulnerability (e.g., age, disability, ethnic group, sexual orientation, and gender identity) on women's participation and access to resources and opportunities.

(ii) gender gap in participation and attainment in education, including in vocational training;

(iii) gender segregation in the formal and informal economy (labor market and enterprises);

(iv) unequal access to health care; and

(v) high rates of gender-based violence.

The GMS Gender Strategy proposes to address the identified gender barriers and achieve the three objectives through

- **mainstreaming gender equality in the *thematic sectors*,**
- **integrating a gender equality element in *relevant GMS Regional Investment Framework (RIF) projects*, and**
- **incorporating gender equality principles and objectives into the six *crosscutting themes* of gender mainstreaming, as relevant to the GMS Program's sectors, projects, and other events.**

Echoing the GMS-2030, the GMS Gender Strategy acknowledges the compounding effects of the intersection of gender inequality with other dimensions of discrimination and vulnerability on women's participation and access to resources and opportunities.[30] As stated in the executive summary of the Gender Strategy, "the assessment found that gender inequalities were compounded by other social categorizations, including, but not limited to, disability, age, location (rural or urban), or sexual orientation."[31] Other sources of discrimination and vulnerability explicitly mentioned in other sections of the Gender Strategy are socioeconomic status, ethnicity, and gender identity.

OBJECTIVES

As mentioned in section I, the GMS 2030 Gender Strategy has three objectives:

(i) Improve existing methods and develop new and innovative approaches to gender mainstreaming to ensure equal access, participation, and treatment in opportunities arising from the GMS Program;

(ii) Complement subregional efforts to explicitly address barriers affecting the full participation of women and men of all ages and abilities in all socioeconomic spheres; and

(iii) Address pervasive gender norms that disadvantage one group over another.

---

[30] The intersectional analysis highlights the diversity of women's situations and posits that women experience the barriers to equal participation and access to resources and opportunities in different degrees depending on the extent to which the different dimensions of inequality, discrimination, and vulnerability intersect in their lives. For instance, women with disabilities, older women, women belonging to minority ethnic groups, women with diverse or "nonconforming" sexual orientation and gender identity, income-poor women, and women in difficult geographic locations (e.g., remote areas prone to disasters triggered by natural hazards) are less likely to participate and access available resources and opportunities.

[31] Footnote 1, p. vi.

Figure 3. Objectives of the Greater Mekong Subregion Gender Strategy

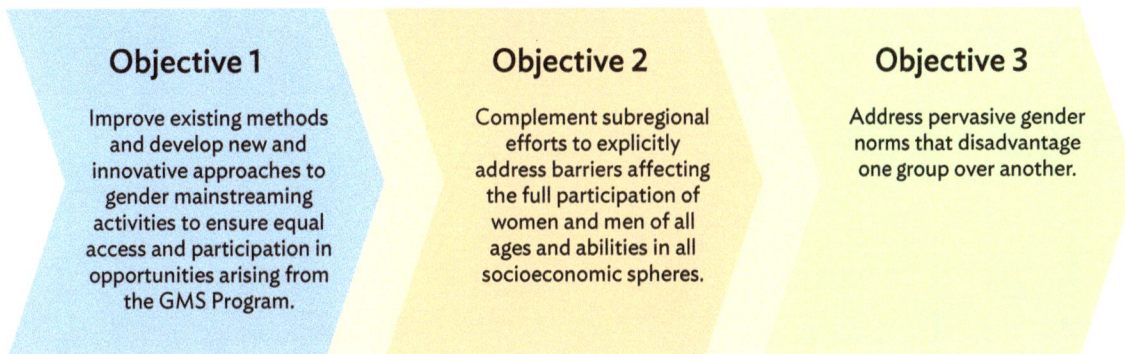

Objective 1

Improve existing methods and develop new and innovative approaches to gender mainstreaming activities to ensure equal access and participation in opportunities arising from the GMS Program.

Objective 2

Complement subregional efforts to explicitly address barriers affecting the full participation of women and men of all ages and abilities in all socioeconomic spheres.

Objective 3

Address pervasive gender norms that disadvantage one group over another.

GMS = Greater Mekong Subregion.

Source: ADB. 2022. *Greater Mekong Subregion Gender Strategy*. p. 5.

The three objectives of the GMS Gender Strategy (Figure 3), while separate and self-contained, mutually support each other. The achievement of the first objective will strengthen the GMS Program's capacity to complement subregional efforts to address gender barriers experienced by women and men of all ages and abilities (and disabilities) in all socioeconomic spheres, especially those experiencing multiple disadvantages due to intersecting vulnerabilities (e.g., older women and women with disabilities who are income-poor). The achievement of the first two objectives will enable the GMS Program to actively address pervasive gender barriers that disadvantage one group over another. Then, initiatives for the third objective will serve as a driving force to achieve the first and second objectives.

GENDER MAINSTREAMING ENTRY POINTS

The GMS Gender Strategy proposes to address the identified gender barriers and challenges (summarized in section II) and achieve the three objectives (stated in sections I and II) through (i) mainstreaming gender equality in

The emphasis of actions can range:

- from a specific *focus on women's and girls' empowerment*
- to the *recognition of intersectionality as an analytical framework* to capture multiple dimensions of discrimination and vulnerability
- to *expanded definitions of gender discrimination* that encompass men, women, and people whose gender identity differs from their sex assigned at birth.

the thematic sectors, (ii) integrating a gender equality element in relevant projects under the GMS RIF, and (iii) incorporating gender equality principles and objectives into six crosscutting themes that may be relevant to GMS Program's sectors, projects, and other events. This implementation plan follows and focuses on these three entry points.

The GMS Program's eight thematic sectors, which are grouped into three pillars—are (i) health cooperation and (ii) environmental

Minorities and older women. A group of women from Honghe Prefecture in Yunnan Province access clean and convenient tap water. The Greater Mekong Subregion Gender Strategy recognizes the intersection of gender inequality with other dimensions of discrimination and vulnerability, like age and ethnicity, among others.

sustainability and climate change under the community pillar; (iii) transport and (iv) energy under the connectivity pillar; and (v) trade and investment, (vi) agriculture, (vii) tourism, and (viii) urban development under the competitiveness pillar (Figure 1). Most of these sectors have incorporated gender elements into their strategic frameworks and action plans in different degrees. The assessment and strengthening of these elements are among the major goals of this GSIP.

The projects under the RIF refer to multi-country regional projects or single-country projects with regional economic benefits.[32] In a joint statement at the 7th GMS Summit in 2021, the GMS Leaders mandated the GMS ministers and senior officials to develop a realistic and implementable pipeline of projects that support the strategic and operational priorities of GMS-2030. To be included in the GMS RIF, a project should meet the minimum criteria[33] and may also consider additional aspirational

---

[32]   GMS Secretariat. 2022. *Regional Investment Framework 2023–2025*.

[33]   The minimum criteria are (i) meet basic identification project criteria, (ii) have a regional impact or spillover effect; (iii) supported by active sectors of cooperation under the GMS program (e.g., proposed through an active working group mechanisms); (iv) aligns with GMS regional and/or national and sector strategies; and (v) if applicable, may include minimum standards of project readiness, such as strong ownership, a clear sponsor, completed project preparation stages (e.g., feasibility study), identified source of financing, and included in national investment plans.

criteria. As "has gender elements" is one of the aspirational criteria,[34] it may or may not be considered a criterion for project selection. This GSIP proposes to make "has strong gender elements" a minimum criterion for projects that are relevant to gender or can contribute to gender equality as assessed by the Task Force on Gender, which will be formed under this GSIP.

The six crosscutting themes of gender entry points, according to the Gender Strategy, are (i) macroeconomic coordination, (ii) labor mobility and safe migration, (iii) education and skills, (iv) special economic zones, (v) digitalization, and (vi) gender norms and attitudes or gender-based violence. These themes were drawn from the list of "Other Areas of Cooperation" of the GMS-2030.[35] The Gender Strategy provides examples of gender-related actions that can be undertaken for each of these themes (summarized in Appendix 2 of this GSIP). Furthermore, the GSIP proposes considering these themes when designing the GMS Program's gender forums.

According to the Gender Strategy, the approach to mainstreaming gender will be based on the results of the GMS gender assessment, implemented flexibly, and tailored at the project level to respond to evolving national gender equality regulatory frameworks, policies, and practices in the GMS countries. It states that "the emphasis can range from a specific focus on women and girls' empowerment to the recognition of intersectionality as an analytical framework to capture multiple dimensions of discrimination and vulnerability, including gender, age, socioeconomic status, and

expanded definitions of gender discrimination that encompass men and women, as well as people whose gender identity differs from their sex assigned at birth."[36]

The GMS countries may not be at the same level or pace in responding to issues of discrimination against people with diverse sexual orientations and gender identities and expressions (SOGIE). Given this situation, the support for related gender mainstreaming actions (along the stated three entry points) will be country-specific (informed by the country's sociocultural values and practices and legal framework), demand-driven (with the involvement of government partners), and flexible (considering the country's readiness or pace and approaches in responding to SOGIE issues). For instance, Thailand legally recognizes people with diverse SOGIE. Its Gender Equality Act B.E. 2558 covers a person who "expresses themselves differently from their inborn gender."[37] In recognition of this national gender policy, this implementation plan, in line with the GMS Gender Strategy, may support projects with gender features benefiting people with diverse sexual orientations, gender identities and expressions, and sex characteristics (SOGIESC), submitted for inclusion in the GMS Program RIF.

IMPLEMENTATION MECHANISMS

The GMS Gender Strategy identifies four collaborative implementation mechanisms (i.e., policy dialogue, capacity development, knowledge products, and pilot projects)

---

[34] Initially there were five aspirational criteria; this has now been expanded to eight. The aspirational criteria are (i) aligns with standards for quality infrastructure, (ii) is a multi-country project with regional benefits, (iii) fosters digitalization, (iv) supports spatial development (economic corridors and/or city clusters), (v) has private sector participation, (vi) has a specific and targeted impact on poor people, (vii) has gender elements, and (viii) is a green project or support the blue economy. This RIF states that projects "may include one or more aspirational criteria."

[35] Footnote 17, p. 36, para. 128.

[36] Footnote 1, p. 1, para. 4.

[37] Government of Thailand. 2015. *Thailand Gender Equality Act. B.E. 2558*

Figure 4: Implementation Mechanisms of the Greater Mekong Subregion Gender Strategy

Gender Entry Points Across

Crosscutting Themes

Extracted from
GMS-2030—macroeconomic coordination,
education and skills, labor mobility and safe
migration, digitalization, and SEZs,
including gender-based violence.

Sectors

Identified under Community: health and
climate change; Connectivity: transport
and energy; and Competitiveness: trade
and investment, agriculture, tourism and
urban development.

**Projects: Regional
Investment Framework**

Policy
Dialogue

Thematic
Forums and
Roundtables

Sector
Forums with
GMS
Working
Groups

Potential
GMS Task
Force on
Gender

Capacity
Building

Knowledge
Products

Pilot
Projects

GMS = Greater Mekong Subregion, SEZ = special economic zone.

Source: ADB. 2022. *Greater Mekong Subregion Gender Strategy*. p. 15.

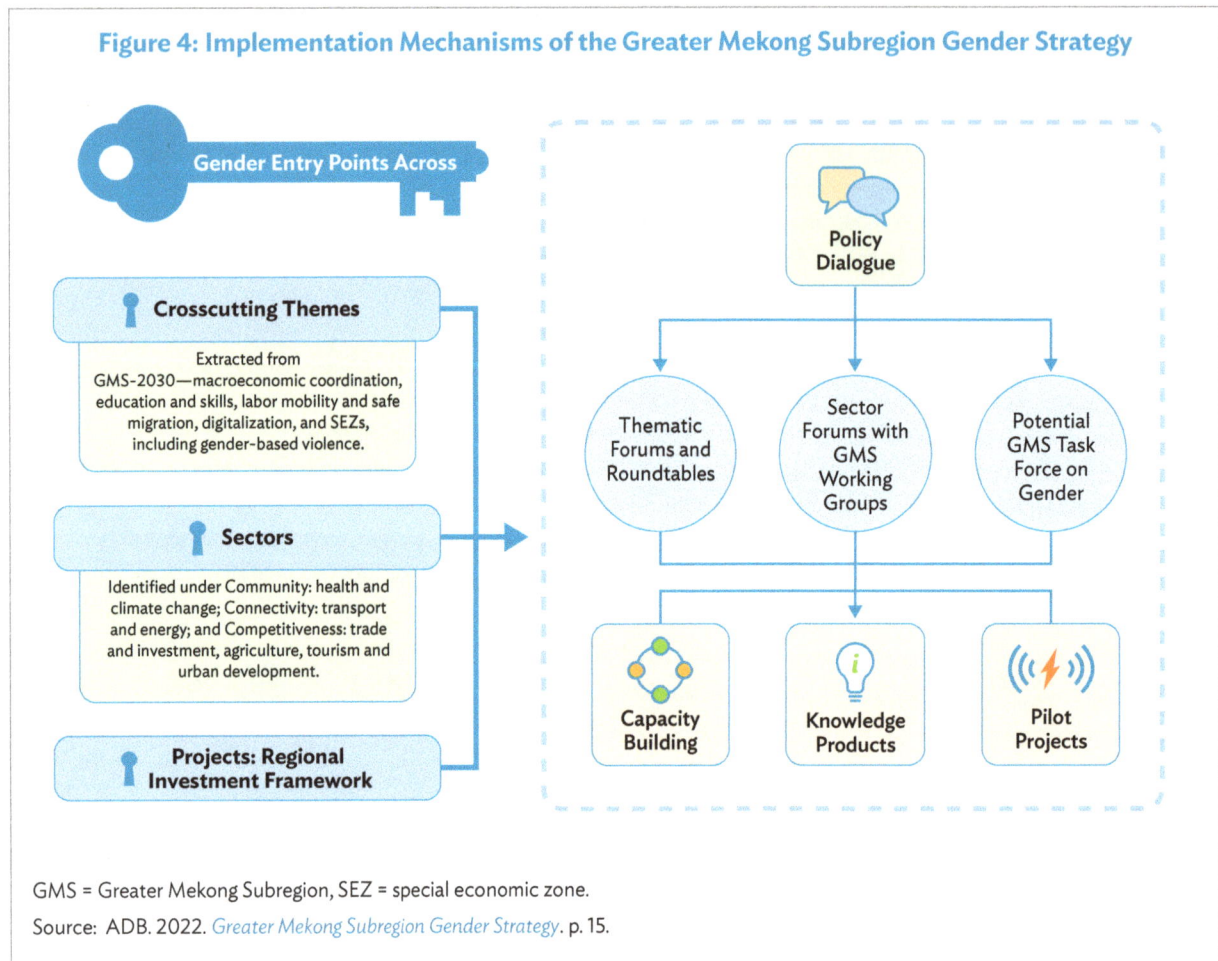

to mainstream gender in the GMS Gender Strategy's crosscutting themes, GMS-2030 sectors, and GMS RIF projects (Figure 4; Figure 3 in the Gender Strategy). The activities in the GSIP reflect these mechanisms.

RESULTS FRAMEWORK

To monitor and measure the progress and results of gender equality initiatives across the GMS Program pillars, sectors, and RIF projects, the GMS Gender Strategy proposes integrating gender performance indicators—at the input, output, and outcome levels—into the GMS-2030 Results Framework, rather than in a separate gender-specific evaluation document.[38] The Gender Strategy contends that integrating gender equality within the broader GMS-2030 Results Framework will support the effective integration of gender equality in all program activities. However, as the GMS-2030 Results Framework was completed before the development of the Gender Strategy, the possible gender indicators listed in the appendix of the Gender Strategy[39] were not integrated. As stated in Section II, this implementation plan proposes

---

[38]   Footnote 1, p. 18, para. 96.
[39]   Footnote 1, p. 20, Appendix.

to revisit the gender performance indicators of the GMS-2030 Results Framework during its midterm review (MTR) for clarification and refinement. The MTR of the GMS-2030 Results Framework would be an opportunity to include the possible gender indicators of the Gender Strategy.

This GSIP combines the gender performance indicators of the GMS-2030 Results Framework and the possible indicators in the appendix of the Gender Strategy to define the outcome and output indicators of the activities for developing the capacity of the GMS Program to achieve the three objectives of the Gender Strategy (footnote 39).

The GMS Gender Strategy proposes integrating gender performance indicators at the input, output, and outcome levels into the GMS-2030 Results Framework rather than having a separate gender-specific evaluation document.

Policy dialogue and Gender Strategy Implementation Plan. Villagers near the Nakai Reservoir, Lao People's Democratic Republic, participate in a training program under the Greater Mekong Subregion Nam Theun 2 Hydroelectric Project. Policy dialogue is one of five institutional activities under GSIP to mainstream gender in sectoral frameworks, operations, and Regional Investment Framework projects.

3

THE GENDER STRATEGY IMPLEMENTATION PLAN 2025–2030

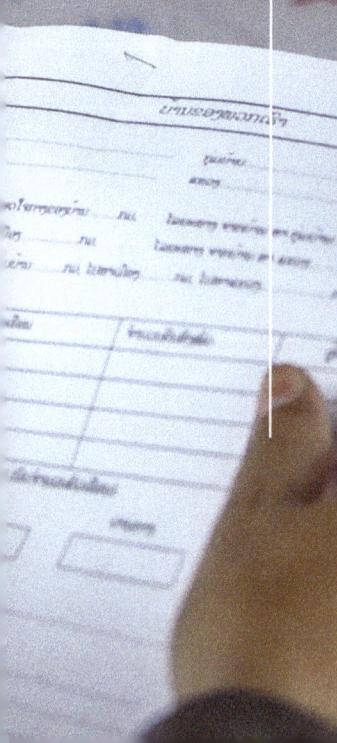

The GSIP provides the specific, measurable or observable, attainable, relevant, and time-bound (SMART) activities and target outputs and defines the gender performance indicators at the output, outcome, and impact levels of the Gender Strategy. Figure 5 encapsulates them in a theory of change. The three objectives of the Gender Strategy, presented in a modified form, are shown as outcomes in Figure 5.

Figure 5: Greater Mekong Subregion Program Gender Strategy Implementation Plan: Theory of Change

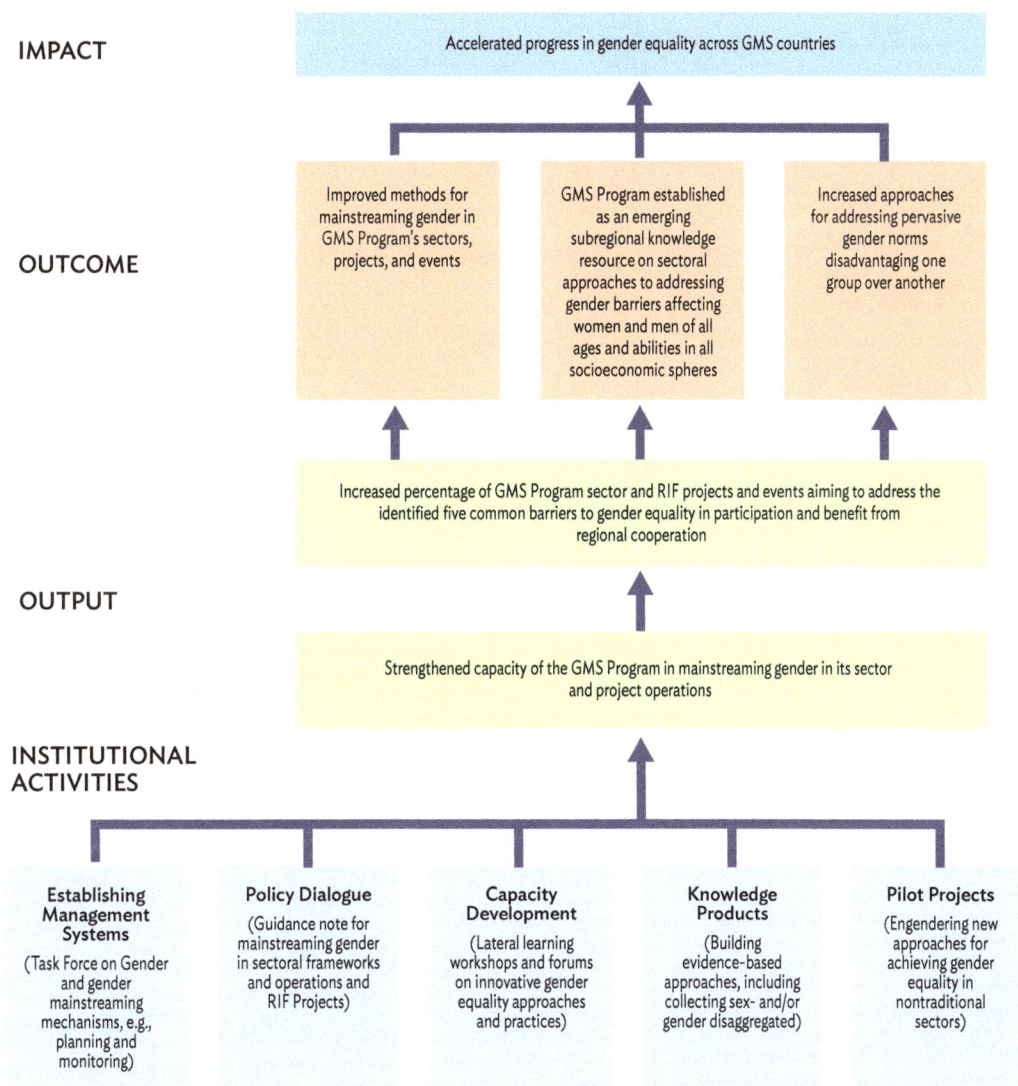

IMPACT

Accelerated progress in gender equality across GMS countries

OUTCOME

Improved methods for mainstreaming gender in GMS Program's sectors, projects, and events

GMS Program established as an emerging subregional knowledge resource on sectoral approaches to addressing gender barriers affecting women and men of all ages and abilities in all socioeconomic spheres

Increased approaches for addressing pervasive gender norms disadvantaging one group over another

Increased percentage of GMS Program sector and RIF projects and events aiming to address the identified five common barriers to gender equality in participation and benefit from regional cooperation

OUTPUT

Strengthened capacity of the GMS Program in mainstreaming gender in its sector and project operations

INSTITUTIONAL ACTIVITIES

Establishing Management Systems
(Task Force on Gender and gender mainstreaming mechanisms, e.g., planning and monitoring)

Policy Dialogue
(Guidance note for mainstreaming gender in sectoral frameworks and operations and RIF Projects)

Capacity Development
(Lateral learning workshops and forums on innovative gender equality approaches and practices)

Knowledge Products
(Building evidence-based approaches, including collecting sex- and/or gender disaggregated)

Pilot Projects
(Engendering new approaches for achieving gender equality in nontraditional sectors)

GMS = Greater Mekong Subregion, RIF = Regional Investment Framework.

a Based on the results of the gender assessment conducted in 2020, the five common barriers to gender equality in participation and benefit from regional cooperation across the GMS countries are (i) social norms that assign individuals to specific gender roles, (ii) gender gap in participation and attainment in education, including in vocational training; (iii) gender segregation in the formal and informal economy (labor market and enterprises); (iv) unequal access to health care; and (v) high rates of gender-based violence.

Source: GMS Program.

The Gender Strategy Implementation Plan has four sets of activities.

- **The first set aims at establishing the management system (Task Force on Gender) for delivering the plan.**
- **The three other sets aim at developing the GMS Program's capacity to achieve the three Gender Strategy objectives.**

The implementation plan has the following four sets of activities:

(i) Activities that aim to establish the management systems, including the formation of a Task Force on Gender, for delivering the GSIP.

(ii) Activities that aim to strengthen the integration of gender equality principles and approaches into the frameworks and operations of the GMS Program's eight sectors and the RIF projects.

(iii) Activities that aim to build the GMS Program's knowledge base in promoting gender equality through an intersectionality lens (looking at how gender inequality intersects with other sources of discrimination and vulnerabilities, such as age and ability or disability) and establish the GMS Program

The implementation plan for Gender Strategy Objective 1 focuses on improving the GMS Program's methods for mainstreaming gender in the:

- **Strategic framework and operations of the eight GMS sectors and**
- **GMS RIF Projects.**

as an emerging knowledge resource in mainstreaming gender in regional cooperation initiatives.

(iv) Additional activities to expand the knowledge base on gender mainstreaming approaches through pilot projects and gender forums on emerging issues and initiatives to be held every 3 years.

The second to fourth sets of activities begin with a gender assessment, and the subsequent activities are based on the results of this assessment. This ensures that the GSIP approaches are evidence-based. Appendix 3 provides an overview of the GSIP's activities in a Gantt chart.

MANAGEMENT SYSTEMS FOR DELIVERING THE IMPLEMENTATION PLAN

The GSIP begins with the formation of the GMS Task Force on Gender, which will be primarily responsible for (i) leading, supervising, and monitoring the quality delivery of the GMS GSIP; (ii) guiding the sector working groups in assessing and addressing gaps in mainstreaming gender in the sector strategic frameworks and action plans; (iii) identifying RIF pipeline projects that can contribute to gender equality and reviewing these projects to ensure that they comply with the GMS guidelines for integrating gender in relevant projects (to be developed under this implementation plan); and (iv) aligning the delivery of the GSIP with ongoing national gender strategies and plans. It will be composed of two representatives (national gender-focal persons) from each GMS country and will ensure that the delivery of the GSIP is in line with ongoing national gender strategies and plans. The national gender focal persons may come from the gender ministries of the countries. The GMS Secretariat, which

Women in the trade sector. A woman sits in front of her fruit store, which has benefited from an influx of customers thanks to the Greater Mekong Subregion Route 3. This project has provided many opportunities to Thais living along the route to increase their income.

is based in the Regional Cooperation Division of the Asian Development Bank Southeast Asia Department, will assist the Task Force by providing staff and/or consultant support in performing these functions. The GMS Secretariat will also assist the task force on Gender in ensuring that the GSIP will be reflected in or aligned with ADB's country partnership strategy for each GMS country.[40]

The Task Force on Gender will conduct a midterm review in the last quarter of 2027 and a terminal review at its completion in the last quarter of 2030 to assess the achievement of the GSIP.

GENDER STRATEGY OBJECTIVE 1

Improve existing methods and develop new and innovative approaches to gender mainstreaming to ensure equal access, participation, and treatment in opportunities arising from the GMS Program

The existing methods and approaches mentioned in the objective are those of the GMS Program. The specific activities and outputs aimed at improving these methods include: (i) integrating gender equality elements into the sectors' strategic frameworks, action plans, and operations; and (ii) including "has gender

---

[40]   The Task Force on Gender, with the support of the GMS Secretariat, may consider adding to this GSIP other promising approaches in gender mainstreaming from existing national gender mainstreaming strategies and action plans, such as the *Country Gender Equality and Women's Empowerment Plan* in ADB's country partnership strategy 2024–2028 for the Lao PDR.

elements" in the list of aspirational criteria for the GMS RIF projects.[41] Section III, subsection B, points 1 and 2 provide an overview of the status of these methods, which informed this GSIP's actions for Objective 1.

Gender Elements of the Sectors' Strategic Frameworks and Action Plans

A general assessment of the gender equality elements of the strategic frameworks of eight sectors (prior to the formulation of this GSIP) shows commendable efforts in mainstreaming gender, but these efforts are uneven across sectors (Table 1; the reasons for the "substantially, partially, or no" assessment are in Appendix 4). This unevenness indicates the need to assess and improve the sectors' existing methods for gender mainstreaming. An in-depth gender assessment is needed to validate and expand the general assessment in Table 1 and Appendix 4. Preparing guidance notes, engaging gender specialists, and providing training may improve current practices.

Table 1: Gender Mainstreaming in Recent Strategic Frameworks of Eight Greater Mekong Subregion Sectors

Greater Mekong Subregion Program Sectors	Period Covered by the Reviewed Strategic Framework or Strategy Paper	Key Areas for Gender Mainstreaming			
		Is sector gender analysis (including relevant sex or gender-disaggregated data) provided?	Is advancing gender equality explicit in the principles and objectives?	Is gender mainstreaming explicit in the approaches and implementation structures?	Are gender equality indicators explicit in the results framework?
1. Agriculture	2018–2022[a]	No	Substantially	Substantially	Substantially
2. Energy	2015–2020[b]	No	No	No	No
3. Environmental sustainability and climate change	2018–2022[c]	Partially	Partially	Partially	Partially
4. Health	2019–2023[d]	Partially	Substantially	Substantially	Substantially
5. Transport	2018–2030[e]	No	No	No	No
6. Tourism	2016–2025[f]	Partially	Substantially	Partial	No
7. Trade and investment	N/A	N/A No strategic framework			
8. Urban development	2015–2022[g]	Partially	Substantially	No	No

N/A = not applicable.

[a] Asian Development Bank (ADB). 2018. *Strategy for Promoting Safe and Environment-Friendly Agro-Based Value Chains in the Greater Mekong Subregion and Siem Reap Action Plan, 2018–2022*.
[b] ADB. 2016. *Greater Mekong Subregion Energy Sector Assessment, Strategy, and Roadmap*.
[c] GMS Environment Operations Center, Asian Development Bank. 2017. *Greater Mekong Subregion Core Environment Program Strategic Framework and Action Plan 2018–2022*.
[d] ADB. 2019. *Greater Mekong Subregion Health Cooperation Strategy 2019–2023*.
[e] ADB. 2018. *GMS Transport Sector Strategy 2030: Toward a Seamless, Efficient, Reliable, and Sustainable GMS Transport System*.
[f] Mekong Tourism Coordinating Office. 2017. *Greater Mekong Subregion Tourism Sector Strategy 2016–2025*.
[g] ADB. 2015. *Greater Mekong Subregion Urban Development Strategic Framework 2015–2022*.

Source: GMS Secretariat.

---

[41]   GMS Secretariat. 2022. *Regional Investment Framework 2023–2025*.

To help strengthen and expand the gender features of the sectors' strategic frameworks, action plans, and practices, the GSIP includes two sets of 2-day capacity development programs in gender mainstreaming to be conducted every 3 years: one for the sector working groups under GMS Program pillars 1 and 2 (i.e., health, environmental sustainability and climate change, transport, and energy) and another for the sector working groups under pillar 3 (i.e., trade and investment facilitation, agriculture, tourism, and urban development). These capacity development programs will be in the form of lateral learning workshops, where the participants learn from each other by sharing analyses and reflections on the global and regional situation, challenges, and trends in gender equality across sectors and exchanging experiences, good practices, and lessons. This learning exchange is expected to surface or highlight novel and effective techniques for incorporating gender equality principles within the operations of each of the eight sectors. The goal is to ensure equal opportunities to participate and access the benefits of regional cooperation.

To align the capacity development programs with the collective aspirations of the GMS countries and ensure their responsiveness to each country's needs and priorities, the GMS Task Force on Gender, to be composed of representatives from the GMS countries, will lead the designing of the lateral learning workshops and program of activities in consultation with the national secretariats and sector working groups.

Gender Elements of the GMS Regional Investment Framework Projects

As mentioned in section II, the RIF lists "has gender elements" as one of the aspirational criteria that may be selected for a project. As the RIF and GMS-2030 Results Framework

Gender mainstreaming is uneven within each of the sectors and across the eight sectors.

Uneven gender mainstreaming within a sector means gender is not integrated into all key parts of the sector's strategic frameworks and action plans.

Uneven gender mainstreaming across sectors means that some sectors have substantive gender elements, while other sectors have none.

The GSIP proposes to conduct an in-depth assessment of the sector's gender mainstreaming methods to validate this assessment and cover the operations and practices of the eight sector working groups.

state that a project may include one or more of the eight aspirational criteria (footnote 34), "has gender elements" may not be one of them. To increase the number of RIF projects with gender elements, the GSIP proposes making this aspirational criterion a minimum criterion for projects that the Task Force on Gender (with the assistance of the GMS Secretariat) may deem relevant to gender or can contribute to gender equality.

In addition, revisiting and strengthening the gender-related indicators of the GMS-2030 Results Framework is crucial in increasing the number of GMS RIF projects that promote gender equality.[42] The GMS Results Framework has three levels of results indicators:

(i) **Level 1.** Regional Development Context, which assesses the progress of the GMS subregion toward attaining GMS-2030 vision by providing data on macro-level

---

[42] GMS Secretariat. 2022. *The Greater Mekong Subregion Program Strategy 2030 Results Framework*. Tables 2 and 3, pp. 10–12.

Mainstreaming gender in Greater Mekong Subregion projects. A seminar is conducted for villagers under the Tonle Sap Rural Water Supply and Sanitation Project in Cambodia.

indicators that reflect the impact of the GMS Program initiatives and other multiple factors at the national, subregional or regional, and global levels;

(ii) **Level 2.** Sector and Subsector Outcomes and Outputs, which measure the results of regional cooperation and integration initiatives under the three pillars of GMS-2030;

(iii) **Level 3.** Institutional Effectiveness, which tracks the overall effectiveness of the GMS Program's institutions, success in generating and mobilizing resources, and delivering quality knowledge relevant to the program needs by measuring indicators grouped into three categories: (a) Level 3a pertains to the knowledge products and services that aim to enhance the quality of interventions and results; (b) Level 3b pertains to the performance

of the RIF that addresses programming and project selection and processes; and (c) Level 3c covers the institutional mechanisms of the GMS Program.

Gender equality results indicators are explicit in Levels 2 and 3 as follows:

(i) **Level 2 (Sector and Subsector Outcomes and Outputs) Crosscutting Theme 1** "GMS investment projects that effectively mainstream gender in their design (%)" with a target of 50% and a baseline of 33% in 2019–2021.[43]

(ii) **Level 3b (Programming, project quality, and RIF processes):**
(a) **Regional Investment Framework 1.** "A new RIF prepared to develop a compendium of projects eligible for financing from a variety of public and

---

43   In ADB's Guidelines for Gender Mainstreaming of ADB Projects, *gender equity theme and effective gender mainstreaming* are the top two categories in the project gender categorization system. A project is gender equity theme-categorized if it has a performance indicator at the outcome level, performance indicators in at least 50% of the outputs, and a gender action plan. *Effective gender mainstreaming*-categorized projects have the same features except for the requirement to have an outcome performance indicator.

private sources, emphasizing project quality, sustainability, and advancing gender equality and social inclusion."

(b) **Regional Investment Framework 3.** "Generation of gender-disaggregated data to be promoted in the new RIF."

(c) **Regional Investment Framework 5.** "At least 50% of RIF projects fulfill at least three aspirational criteria identified in the new RIF by 2030." This statement is now adjusted to the expanded eight aspirational criteria. "Has gender elements" is still one of the eight aspirational criteria.

In addition to incorporating gender indicators in relevant Level 1 impact indicators, the GSIP proposes clarifying and refining the Levels 2 and 3 gender-related indicators. Questions to ask are as follows:

(i) What does "advancing gender equality and social inclusion" under Regional Investment Framework 1 mean? When does a project advance gender equality and social inclusion?

(ii) What does "generation of gender-disaggregated data" under Regional Investment Framework 3 mean?[44] How is it different from generating sex-disaggregated data?

(iii) What are the criteria to say that a project effectively mainstreamed gender in its design (Level 2, Cross-cutting Theme 1)?

The GSIP presents three sets of activities to improve the GMS Program's methods for mainstreaming gender in RIF projects:

- Making *"has strong gender elements"* a *minimum criterion* for gender-relevant RIF projects.
- *Developing a guidance note* (which can eventually be transformed as a common guideline) for:
  - identifying gender-relevant projects;
  - designing the gender features of projects; and
  - evaluating the project's gender impacts.
- Revisiting and *strengthening the project gender performance indicators* of the GMS Results Framework.

Guidance Note for Mainstreaming Gender in GMS Regional Investment Framework Projects

Amending the GMS-2030 Results Framework and the GMS Regional Investment Framework may not be feasible before the midterm review of the GMS Strategic Framework 2030, which is expected in 2026 or 2027. As a stopgap measure, a guidance note for improving the existing methods for mainstreaming gender in RIF projects may be developed by the Task Force on Gender with the assistance of the GMS

---

44   As the GMS Results Framework does not define gender-disaggregated data and its difference from sex-disaggregated data, this Gender Strategy Implementation Plan offers a differentiation for reference when revising and enhancing the Results Framework's gender-related indicators. The terms sex-disaggregated data and gender-disaggregated data are used interchangeably in many documents. However, their focus may differ. Sex-disaggregated data are typically collected based on people's assigned sex at birth or two biological categories: males and females. On the other hand, gender-disaggregated data may include a category or categories for people whose gender identity is different from the sex assigned to them at birth, such as transgender men and transgender women. There are countries in the world, such as Bangladesh, India, and Nepal, that legally recognize and incorporate in their official documents a "third gender" identity and, thus, use gender-disaggregated data. However, the adoption or non-adoption of gender-disaggregated data for specific GMS RIF projects will follow the country's national gender framework, policies, and practices. This implementation plan uses gender-disaggregated data as it is the term used in the GMS Results Framework, which was approved or endorsed by the GMS Leaders. For more information on the differences between sex-disaggregated and gender-disaggregated data, refer to R. Colaco and S. Watson-Grant. 2021. *A Global Call for Action for Gender-Inclusive Data Collection and Use: Policy Brief. RTI Press.*

Secretariat. This guidance note could be adopted from similar documents (of development partners or regional networks) or could be a harmonized version of the guidelines for gender mainstreaming in projects of the GMS countries and development partners. While ADB, which houses and supports the GMS Secretariat, has clear guides for assessing a project's gender design features and gender equality results at completion,[45] the GMS Secretariat cannot unilaterally use them to assess GMS RIF projects that other development partners finance. These guidelines must result from policy dialogue and

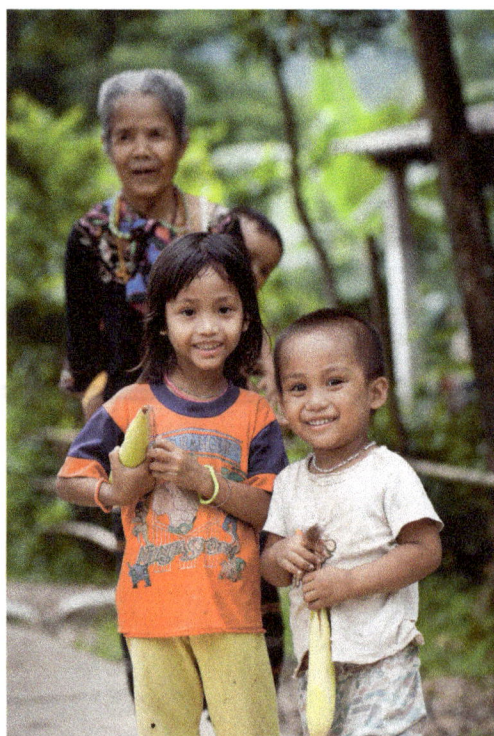

Generations of Van Kieu. Local facilities for ethnic people in Mo O commune, Viet Nam, have been supported by ADB-financed projects. The Gender Strategy Implementation Plan seeks to improve methods for mainstreaming gender in Greater Mekong Subregion projects.

be agreed on by the GMS countries' gender focal points and the GMS development partners for uniform adoption across RIF projects.

The guidance note will serve as the reference for the following:

(i) Identifying RIF projects that are relevant to gender or can contribute to gender equality;
(ii) Conducting a gender analysis to inform the project's gender features;
(iii) Conducting stakeholder analysis to identify key groups (government agencies, civil society organizations, private sector or business organizations, and development partners) involved in mainstreaming gender in projects and ways to involve them effectively;
(iv) Assessing when a project design has "strong gender elements"—defining both the terms "strong" and "gender elements;"
(v) Integrating gender into each phase of the project development cycle—from planning and budgeting (gender-responsive budgeting), implementation, and monitoring to evaluation at completion; and
(vi) Evaluating and reporting the project's gender equality results at mid-term and completion.

The guidance note will include tips, checklists, and tools for mainstreaming gender in sector projects for each of the eight sectors of the GMS Program.[46] The Task Force on Gender may convert this guidance note into a common guideline for mainstreaming gender in RIF projects even after their MTR when the GMS Results Framework and GMS Regional Investment Framework have been enhanced.

---

[45]   ADB. 2021. *Guidelines for Gender Mainstreaming Categories of ADB Projects*; ADB. 2022. *Guidelines for the At-Exit Assessment of Gender Equality Results of ADB Projects*.

[46]   Examples of checklists for sectoral projects can be found in the *Harmonized Gender and Development Guidelines for Project Development, Implementation, Monitoring and Evaluation* used by the Official Development Assistance-Gender and Development Network in the Philippines. Reference: National Economic and Development Authority, Philippine Commission on Women, and Official Development Assistance Gender and Development Network. 2016. *Harmonized Gender and Development Guidelines for Project Development, Implementation, Monitoring and Evaluation*.

GENDER STRATEGY OBJECTIVE 2

Complement subregional efforts to explicitly address gender barriers affecting the full participation of individuals of all ages and abilities in all socioeconomic spheres

While the focus of the activities for the first objective is strengthening the GMS Program's internal operational frameworks, systems, and mechanisms for gender mainstreaming, the second objective looks outward to learn from and link with other subregional efforts (at the national and subregional levels by government agencies, civil society organizations, private sector or business organizations, and multilateral and bilateral development agencies) promoting gender equality for complementation (Table 2). Table 3 provides the initial steps to develop the capacity of the GMS Program to engage in this level of action. These steps begin with an assessment of the following:

(i) issues faced by women and men, especially those experiencing intersecting disadvantaged identities (e.g., older women of minority ethnic groups and young women with disabilities of low education and income levels), in the GMS countries and how these issues affect their participation in and benefit from the resources, services, and economic opportunities of the GMS Program;

(ii) current subregional (including national) efforts and good practices to respond to these issues (e.g., by governments, civil society organizations, private sector or business organizations, and bilateral and multilateral development agencies); and

(iii) initiatives by the GMS Program to complement and link with these efforts.

The next steps are to document the GMS Program's (its sectors and select RIF projects) good practices in promoting gender equality and engage in an exchange of good practices with other development organizations in the subregion to build a knowledge base (Table 4).

To develop the GMS Program's capacity to achieve Gender Strategy Objective 2, the GSIP includes three activities:

- **Study the gender barriers experienced by individuals of all ages, abilities (and disabilities), and socio-economic status, especially those experiencing intersecting inequalities and current initiatives of governments, civil society organizations, private sector, and development partners;**
- **Conduct case studies on the GMS Program's good practices and accomplishments in mainstreaming gender in sectors and projects; and**
- **Conduct multi-stakeholder forum on subregional efforts to respond to the intersection of gender inequality with other dimensions of discrimination and vulnerability.**

The implementation plan for developing the capacity of the GMS Program to achieve Objective 3 supplements the actions for Objectives 1 and 2. The objective is to build the GMS Program's knowledge base on innovative gender mainstreaming approaches. It has three sets of activities:

Identifying the priority gender barriers to equal participation and benefit from regional cooperation.

Conducting gender forums on the identified gender barriers every 3 years.

Piloting a project addressing the identified priority gender barrier.

GENDER STRATEGY OBJECTIVE 3

Address pervasive gender norms that disadvantage one group over another

The third objective drives the GMS Program to engage in more innovative actions beyond those for Objectives 1 and 2. The activities aim to expand the GMS Program's knowledge of innovative approaches for addressing pervasive discriminating gender norms. They focus on piloting projects to promote women's visibility and leadership in nontraditional sectors and conducting gender forums on emerging issues and initiatives (Table 5).

Other activities to develop the capacity of the GMS Program to address pervasive discriminating gender norms within its operations (if any) will be designed based on the GSIP's MTR in 2027.

Table 2: Setting Up the Management Systems for Delivering the Greater Mekong Subregion Gender Strategy Implementation Plan

Activities	Description	Performance Indicators and Targets	Means of Verification	Responsible Units	Timeline
1. Form a GMS Task Force on Gender as the main mechanism for leading, supervising, and monitoring the implementation of the GMS Gender Strategy and for disseminating lessons learned	• The task force will consist of two national gender focal persons from each GMS country. • Online meetings will be held once or twice a year to identify gender-relevant projects submitted for inclusion in the RIF and discuss the progress of implementation and results of the gender features of identified projects.	• Criteria for the selection of the GMS Task Force on Gender members developed • Terms of reference of the task force formulated • Task force members identified and assigned • Task force meetings regularly convened	GMS Secretariat's reports	GMS senior officials, with the assistance of the GMS Secretariat, for the formation of the Task Force on Gender	Q1 2025 onward
2. Conduct a review of the GMS GSIP (and achievements) at midterm and completion	The objectives of these meetings are to assess the overall relevance and effectiveness of the GMS GSIP and define the way forward.	Accomplishments, gaps, and lessons from the delivery of the GMS GSIP summed up; remedial actions for problematic activities or targets (if any) addressed	GMS Secretariat's reports	GMS Task Force on Gender, with the assistance of the GMS Secretariat	MTR: Q4 2027 At-Exit: Q4 2030

GMS = Greater Mekong Subregion, GSIP = Gender Strategy Implementation Plan, MTR = midterm review, Q = quarter, RIF = Regional Investment Framework.

Source: GMS Program.

Table 3: Implementation Plan for Developing the Capacity of the Greater Mekong Subregion Program to Achieve the Gender Strategy Objective 1

Output and Activities	Description	Performance Indicators and Targets	Means of Verification	Responsible Units	Timeline
Output 1. Capacity of the sector working groups, committees, and task forces to mainstream gender in their respective sector strategic frameworks strengthened.					
1. Assess each GMS sector's existing methods for gender mainstreaming in-depth.	• This assessment will expand the review done to prepare this GSIP (Table 1 and Appendix 1) to include the actual gender mainstreaming initiatives and practices of the eight sectors. • The assessment will also cover how each sector has engaged private sector/business organizations and civil society organizations in promoting gender equality. • It will also cover the capacity development needs (in gender mainstreaming) of the sector working groups.	• The general gender assessment of sector strategic frameworks and action plans that was done to prepare this implementation plan validated and expanded, and recommendations to develop new and innovative gender mainstreaming approaches provided.	Assessment report	Task Force on Gender and Sector working groups, with the assistance of the GMS Secretariat	Q2–Q3 2025
2. Improve the gender equality features of the eight sectors' strategic frameworks and action plans in line with GMS countries' aspirations.	• Improvements will be based on the results of the assessment done under Activity 1. • The process will be participatory, involving members of the GMS sector working groups and national secretariats (including their gender focal persons). • Guidance for each sector will be provided by gender experts, who will be engaged by the GMS Secretariat in consultation with the Task Force on Gender.	• Improved methods for advancing gender equality are explicitly integrated into the strategic frameworks, action plans, and results frameworks of the eight sectors. • Collection, analysis, and reporting of sex- or gender-disaggregated data explicitly mentioned in the strategic frameworks and action plans. • GMS senior officials endorsed the revised strategic frameworks and plans.	Revised sector strategic framework, action plans, and results framework	Task Force on Gender and sector working groups, with the assistance of the GMS Secretariat	Q4 2025 (four sectors) Q1 2026 (four sectors)
3. Conduct subregional lateral learning workshops on mainstreaming gender in GMS Program pillars 1 and 2 sectors every 3 years.	• The thematic focus of lateral learning will be based on the results of the capacity assessment conducted under Activity 1 and emerging trends in mainstreaming gender in the sectors. • The lateral learning methodology emphasizes learning through sharing of knowledge, practices, and reflections among the participants and resource persons. • Gender experts for each sector will be engaged to guide the designing of the lateral learning modules and facilitate the lateral learning process.	• Lateral learning modules on mainstreaming gender equality in pillars 1 and 2 sectors developed. • At least 80% of the members of pillars 1 and 2 sector working groups reported increased knowledge of approaches for mainstreaming gender in their respective sector strategic frameworks and action plans.	Training or lateral learning evaluation reports	GMS Secretariat guided by the Task Force on Gender and in consultation with the sector working groups	Workshop 1: Q2 2026 Workshop 2: Q2 2029

Continued on next page

Table 3 continued

Output and Activities	Description	Performance Indicators and Targets	Means of Verification	Responsible Units	Timeline
4. Conduct subregional lateral learning workshops on mainstreaming gender equality in pillar 3 sectors every 3 years.		• Lateral learning modules on mainstreaming gender equality in Pillar 3 sectors developed. • At least 80% of the members of pillars 3 sector working groups reported increased knowledge of approaches for mainstreaming gender in their respective sector strategic frameworks and action plans.			Workshop 1: Q2 2026 Workshop 2: Q2 2029
5. Develop a guidance note for designing the gender features and evaluating the gender equality impacts of RIF projects in consultation with GMS stakeholders (including development partners)	• The guidance note will serve as an interim or stopgap measure while awaiting the refinement of the gender features of the GMS-2030 Results Framework and RIF; however, the Task Force on Gender may consider retaining it for continued use. • Existing guidelines for gender mainstreaming related to GMS Program aspirations and operations may be adopted, or existing related guidelines of GMS countries and development partners may be harmonized to develop the guidance note. • Guidance note development will be participatory, involving the GMS sector working groups, national secretariats, GMS development partners, and GMS countries' gender focal points. • Based on the consensus decision of the Task Force on Gender, the guidance note may cover the intersection of gender inequality with other dimensions of discrimination and vulnerability (e.g., age, disability, ethnicity, income status) and gender issues faced by people with diverse SOGIESC.	• GMS national secretariats, sector working groups and task forces, and development partners expressed support for the draft guidance note. • GMS senior officials endorsed the guidance note. • Development agencies/partners agreed to use the guidance note for supported RIF projects. • Mechanisms for reporting RIF projects that effectively mainstream gender in design (including the collection of sex- or gender-disaggregated data) and that effectively completed targeted gender equality results adopted.	Published guidance note	GMS Task Force on Gender, with the assistance of the GMS Secretariat	Q4 2025
6. Transform the RIF projects' aspirational criterion, into a minimum criterion for gender-relevant projects	• The guidance note (developed under Activity 5) will be used as a reference for identifying RIF projects that can contribute to gender equality. • While *"has strong gender elements" will be made a minimum criterion,* a project's specific gender elements (activities, target outputs, and performance indicators) will be designed based on the project's capacity and the baseline data (nature of the sector); therefore, the gender targets should be realistic and attainable.	• "Has strong gender elements" adopted as a minimum criterion for RIF projects that can contribute to gender equality.	Published revised RIF	GMS Task Force on Gender and senior officials, with the assistance of the GMS Secretariat	2026–2027 based on the schedule of the MTR of the RIF

Continued on next page

Table 3 continued

Output and Activities	Description	Performance Indicators and Targets	Means of Verification	Responsible Units	Timeline
7. Refine the gender equality performance indicators at Levels 1, 2, and 3 of the GMS Strategy 2030 Results Framework	• This will be done during the MTR of the GMS-2030 Results Framework. • The proposed refinement of the gender indicators is in the section, Results Framework, of this GSIP.	• Gender equality performance indicators with baseline and targets of the GMS Strategy 2030 Results Framework defined, refined, and expanded. • Revised gender performance indicators of the GMS-2030 Results Framework endorsed by GMS senior officials and ministers.	Published revised GMS Strategy 2030 Results Framework	GMS Task Force on Gender GMS Senior Officials, with the assistance of the GMS secretariat	2026–2027 based on the schedule of the MTR of the GMS-2030 Results Framework

GMS = Greater Mekong Subregion, MTR = midterm review, Q = quarter, RIF = regional investment framework, SOGIESC = sexual orientation, gender identity and expressions, and sex characteristics.

Note: The ADB Strategy 2030 operational priority 2 guidelines and operational plan may be used as a reference for strengthening the gender features of the sectors' strategic frameworks and actions and preparing the guidance note for gender mainstreaming in RIF projects.

Source: GMS Program.

Table 4: Implementation Plan for Developing the Capacity of the Greater Mekong Subregion Program to Achieve the Gender Strategy Objective 2

Outputs and Activities	Description	Performance Indicators and Targets	Means of Verification	Responsible Units	Timeline
Output. GMS Program is positioned as an emerging knowledge resource (through the GMS Program portal) on sectoral approaches to respond to gender barriers affecting the ability of women and men of all ages and abilities in all socioeconomic spheres to participate in and benefit from the GMS regional cooperation initiatives					
1. Conduct a study on the gender barriers experienced by individuals of all ages, abilities (and disabilities) in all socioeconomic spheres (education and income levels, occupations, ethnicity, and geographic location) and initiatives (good practices) in the subregion to address these barriers.	• This study will be undertaken from an intersectionality lens, focusing on women and men experiencing multiple discrimination because of their intersecting disadvantaged identities (e.g., old age, disability, ethnicity, SOGIESC, income status, and geographic location). Specific intersecting issues to highlight in the study will be determined by the Task Force on Gender. • The study will also look at current initiatives of governments, civil society organizations, private sector/business organizations, and development partners in the subregion to respond to intersectionality issues.	• Gender barriers affecting individuals of all ages and abilities (and disabilities) in all socioeconomic spheres identified, and subregional efforts to address these barriers assessed. • GMS Program's initiatives to complement these efforts defined.	Gender diagnostic reports	GMS Secretariat guided by the GMS Task Force on Gender	Q1–Q2 2026

Continued on next page

Table 4 continued

Outputs and Activities	Description	Performance Indicators and Targets	Means of Verification	Responsible Units	Timeline
2. Develop case studies on the GMS Program's good practices and accomplishments in gender mainstreaming (focusing on responses to barriers identified by the study done under Objective 2 Activity #1).	• These case studies will be done at the end of the GSIP period and will focus on the accomplishments of GSIP implementation. • As feasible, one case study per GMS country will be selected.	• Five GMS projects with exemplary practices and achievements in gender mainstreaming presented in a case study report.	Published case study report	GMS Secretariat guided by the GMS Task Force on Gender	Q3–Q4 2029
3. Conduct a multi-stakeholder forum on subregional efforts to respond to the intersection of gender inequality with old age, disabilities, ethnicity, educational and income levels, and geographic location	• The multi-stakeholder forum will be a venue for lateral learning and sharing of practices and resources on addressing the intersection of gender inequality with other dimensions of vulnerability among development organizations in the GMS. • The stakeholders to be invited to the forum are representatives of the government, private sector / business organizations, civil society organizations, and development partners.	• Lessons from various efforts to address barriers to gender equality generated. • The GMS Program presented as a knowledge resource (through the GMS portal) in addressing gender barriers to equal sharing of the benefits of regional cooperation.	Forum report	GMS secretariat, guided by the	GMS Secretariat guided by the GMS Task Force on Gender

GMS = Greater Mekong Subregion, Q = quarter, SOGIESC = sexual orientation, gender identity and expressions, and sex characteristics.

Source: GMS Program.

Table 5: Implementation Plan for Developing the Capacity of the Greater Mekong Subregion Program to Achieve the Gender Strategy Objective 3

Outputs and Activities	Description	Performance Indicators and Targets	Means of Verification	Responsible Units	Timeline
Output. GMS Program's new and innovative measures to address pervasive gender inequality norms developed					
1. Identify the priority gender barriers to equality in participating and accessing the benefits of regional cooperation in GMS countries.	• The objective is to focus the GMS Program's initiatives on the most pressing common needs of the GMS countries. • The priority gender barriers may be drawn from the five common barriers stated in the Gender Strategy or from the GMS Gender Strategy's crosscutting themes.[a] • The bases for the prioritization of gender barriers are (i) national data on the gender situation, (ii) results of consultations with GMS national secretariats (gender focal persons), and (iii) the need to address these barriers at the regional level (no overlap with other regional initiatives).	• Consensus built among the GMS countries on the priority gender issues or themes to be discussed during the GMS Program's gender forums every 3 years. • The focus of the pilot project for promoting women's visibility in nontraditional sectors/industries identified.	GMS Secretariat's Report	Task Force on Gender, with the assistance of the GMS Secretariat	Q3–Q4 2025
2. Conduct gender forums on priority gender issues or themes identified under Activity #1 every 3 years..	• The gender forum held every 3 years will be a venue for sharing analyses of the identified priority issues or themes, existing or emerging good practices, and lessons on innovative measures to be taken by the GMS Program to address pervasive gender inequality norms. • Coordination with other development agencies in the GMS will be done to avoid replicating forums on similar topics.	• Innovative measures to be adopted or undertaken by the GMS Program to address pervasive gender inequality norms identified.	Summary report on the answers of the forum participants on forum evaluation or reflection forms	GMS Secretariat guided by the GMS Task Force on Gender	Forum 1: Q2 2026 Forum 2: Q2 2029
3. Pilot a project for women's empowerment in a nontraditional sector (e.g., energy or transport) at the GMS level.	• The focus of the pilot project will based on the priority issues identified under Activity 1 or on the results of the study done for Objective 2. • The project will also promote the engagement of men and boys in ending toxic masculinities and achieving gender equality and women's empowerment.	• Lessons on innovative measures to promote women's empowerment in nontraditional sectors at the GMS level identified and disseminated through a case study report. • Pilot project's sustainability and expansion plan developed.	Case study reports GMS Secretariat's reports	GMS Task Force on Gender and GMS sector working group of the pilot project, with the assistance of the GMS Secretariat	2027–2030

GMS = Greater Mekong Subregion, GSIP = Gender Strategy Implementation Plan, Q = quarter.

[a] The GMS Gender Strategy's crosscutting themes are (i) macroeconomic coordination, (ii) labor mobility and safe migration, (iii) education and skills development, (iv) special economic zones, (v) digitalization and new technologies, and (vi) gender norms and attitudes, including gender-based violence. Other themes that may also be included are (i) engaging men and boys in ending toxic masculinities and achieving gender equality and women's empowerment, and (ii) addressing discrimination against sexual and gender minorities.

Source: GMS Program.

Women and innovation.
RithSovandalin, from Cambodia,
aims to inspire a generation of female
coders across her country with her
innovative projects.

4
RESULTS
FRAMEWORK

In line with the Gender Strategy, the GSIP does not offer a separate gender-specific evaluation document. Instead, it proposes a list of gender indicators or elements for integration into the three levels of results indicators of the GMS–2030 Results Framework at its mid-term review.[47]

LEVEL 1. REGIONAL DEVELOPMENT CONTEXT: IMPACTS

Implementing the GMS Gender Strategy is expected to contribute to accelerated progress in achieving gender equality across the GMS countries at the subregional level. For the measurement of this impact, this GSIP proposes to incorporate gender equality indicators in the following Level 1 indicators of the GMS-2030 Results Framework:

(i) The proportion of the population (sex-disaggregated) living below nationally determined poverty lines (baseline data to be sex-disaggregated)
(ii) The proportion of the population (sex-disaggregated) living below the $3.20 per day per person international poverty line (baseline data to be sex-disaggregated)
(iii) Income inequality (Gini coefficient) (disaggregated by sex and other categories to be determined by the Task Force on Gender)

These impact indicators will be monitored and measured using evidence-based data and information from the national governments and development partners in the GMS countries.

LEVEL 2. SECTOR AND SUBSECTOR OUTCOMES AND OUTPUTS

The target output of GSIP activities is the strengthened capacity of the GMS Program to gear regional activities for its three pillars (community, connectivity, competitiveness) and RIF projects toward achieving gender equality in sharing the benefits of regional cooperation. The following are the indicators to measure the achievement of this output:

(i) At least 50% of RIF projects address any of the five barriers to gender equality (as identified by the GMS gender assessment) in their design. These barriers are as follows:
(a) social norms that assign individuals to specific gender roles;

In line with the Gender Strategy, the GSIP suggests strengthening the gender performance indicators of the GMS-2030 Results Framework, instead of developing a separate gender-specific evaluation document.

Proposed gender performance indicators are in three levels of the results framework.

The GSIP proposes to incorporate *sector-specific gender equality outcome and output indicators at Level 2 of the GMS-2030 Results Framework. The targets will vary across sectors.* Sectors like agriculture, energy, and transport, where women have lower visibility, are expected to have lower gender targets compared to sectors like education and health, which are traditionally associated with women.

---

[47]   The impact and outcome performance indicators were drawn (with modifications) from the Appendix (Possible Gender Indicators) of the Gender Strategy and the gender indicators of the GMS-2030 Results Framework.

Mainstreaming gender entry points. A woman working in the renewable energy industry. Most GMS sectors, including energy, have incorporated gender elements into their strategic frameworks and action plans. A major goal of the GSIP is to assess and strengthen these elements (photo by iStock.com/ onuma Inthapong).

(b) gender gap in participation and attainment in education, including in vocational training;

(c) gender segregation in the formal and informal economy (labor market and enterprises);

(d) unequal access to health care; and

(e) high rates of gender-based violence.

The specific gender barrier to be addressed will be based on relevance to the project and the priority issues identified during the project's gender and social assessment.

(ii) Percentage of RIF projects reporting successful gender equality results (with gender or sex-disaggregated data) increased by __% (Baseline 2023: XX%)[48]

Monitoring the achievement of these performance indicators implies the need for the Task Force on Gender to review the submitted projects for the RIF (at a specified 3-year period), identify which of these projects can

respond to the gender barriers, and propose related features to be integrated into the project design. The guidance note to be prepared for Objective 1 (Table 3, Output 2) may also require project proponents to specify which gender barrier/s the project seeks to address.

The first output indicator in section IV, subsection B aligns with the GMS-2030 Results Framework Level 2 Croscutting Theme 1 (*GMS initiatives supporting gender equity theme or effective gender mainstreaming enhanced: GMS investment projects that effectively mainstream gender in their design [50%]*). It also aligns with the following possible gender indicators in the GMS Gender Strategy:

(i) Proportion of new GMS projects that incorporate gender-based violence education and prevention activities;

(ii) Number of gender-responsive and inclusive GMS projects supporting women and/or men in nontraditional employment; and

(iii) Number of GMS projects and activities that actively support social and economic inclusion of women from ethnic minorities and women with disabilities.

The second output indicator aligns with the following possible gender indicators of the Gender Strategy:

(i) Percentage of completed projects that met female employment targets; and

(ii) Progress in key health indicators.

The expected outcomes of these outputs are related to the three objectives of the Gender Strategy:

(i) Improved methods for mainstreaming in GMS Program's sectors, projects, and events;

---

[48]   The baseline and indicators will be set in consultation with the Task Force on Gender.

(ii) GMS Program established as an emerging subregional knowledge resource on sectoral approaches to addressing gender barriers affecting women and men of all ages and abilities in all socioeconomic spheres; and

(iii) Increased approaches for addressing pervasive gender norms disadvantaging one group over another.

The GSIP proposes to incorporate sector-specific gender equality outcome and output indicators in the GMS-2030 Results Framework. The indicators will be designed based on the review and enhancement of the eight sectors' strategic frameworks and action plans. The targets will vary across sectors. Sectors like agriculture, energy, and transport, where women have lower visibility, are expected to have lower gender targets than sectors like education and health, which are traditionally associated with women.

LEVEL 3. INSTITUTIONAL EFFECTIVENESS

The Strategy 2030 Results Framework has two explicit gender-related indicators at its Level 3b (programming, project quality, and RIF processes). The GSIP proposes to retain these indicators but with clear operational definitions.

(i) **Regional Investment Framework 1.** "A new RIF prepared to develop a compendium of projects eligible for financing from a variety of public and private sources, emphasizing project quality, sustainability, and advancing gender equality and social inclusion."

(ii) **Regional Investment Framework 3.** "Generation of gender-disaggregated data to be promoted in the new RIF."

As the GSIP proposes to make "has strong gender elements" a minimum criterion for gender-relevant RIF projects, this criterion will no longer be in the list of aspirational criteria for RIF 5 ("By 2030, at least 50% of RIF projects will fulfill at least three aspirational criteria

Jobs for women. Women assemble electronic products in one of the factories inside the Savan Park Special Economic Zone in Savannakhet, Lao People's Democratic Republic.

identified in the new RIF"). Instead, the GMS Program will aim to achieve the first output indicator in section IV, subsection B. For Level 3a (knowledge products and services) and Level 3c (GMS institutions and mechanisms), the GSIP proposes to add "Percentage of GMS events (workshops, meetings, training events) and knowledge products that discuss measures to advance gender equality increased by __% (Baseline 2023: XX%)" (footnote 48). This indicator aligns with the following possible gender indicators of the GMS Gender Strategy:

(i) Number of GMS programs, activities, and initiatives that support sex-disaggregated data collection for the gender equality indicators in the UN SDGs;

(ii) Number of GMS activities that include gender-based violence legal and policy response capacity building;

(iii) Percentage of GMS meetings and workshops that incorporate measures to advance gender equality. These measures include gender balance in speakers and participants, gender thematic activities, and provision of childcare for participants; and

(iv) Number of events or awareness campaigns promoting women from ethnic minorities and women with disabilities.

5

ESTIMATED COST OF FINANCING AND WAY FORWARD

The GMS Gender Strategy Implementation Plan 2025–2030 will require approximately $3.75 million in financing (Table 6).[49]

Table 6: Estimated Cost of the Greater Mekong Subregion Gender Strategy Implementation Plan 2025–2030 (tentative)

Objective and Activity	Indicative Cost ($)
Implementation Plan Management Systems	
1. Formation of the GMS Task Force on Gender	38,000
2. Midterm and terminal (at completion) review of the implementation plan	100,000
Objective 1	
3. Conduct in-depth assessment of each sector's existing methods for gender mainstreaming and enhancement of the gender features of the sector strategic frameworks, action plans, and results framework	160,000
4. Conduct four subregional learning workshops on gender mainstreaming	341,000
5. Develop a guidance note or common guidelines for designing the gender features and assessing the gender equality results of RIF projects • Draft and present the guidelines ($50,000) • Meet with GMS national secretariats and sector working groups and task forces to present the guidelines (virtual) • Conduct partners' forum to discuss the guidelines ($10,000) • Endorse the guidelines at the GMS SOM ($20,000)	80,000
6. Polish the gender equality performance indicators (and targets) of the GMS-2030 Regional Investment Framework	20,000
Objective 2	
7. Conduct study on the gender barriers experienced by individuals of all ages	150,000
8. Conduct five case studies on the GMS Program's good practices and accomplishments in gender equality	100,000
9. Conduct multi-stakeholder forum on subregional efforts	150,000
Objective 3	
10. Conduct two gender forums (2025 and 2028)	100,000
11. Pilot a project for women's employment and leadership in nontraditional sector	2,000,000
12. Coordinate the delivery of the implementation plan (consultant) (5 years)	300,000
Contingency fund (6%)	211,000
Estimated Grand Total	**$3,750,000**

GMS = Greater Mekong Subregion, RIF = Regional Investment Framework, SOM = Senior Officials Meeting.
Note: See Appendix 3 for a list of Gender Strategy Implementation Plan activities.
Source: GMS Secretariat.

A critical way forward is sustaining the coordination and communication with the GMS national and sector gender focal persons to keep abreast of the gender situation and trends in the subregion. The degree of collaboration of the key players of the GMS Program, including the RIF project teams, in delivering this implementation plan will be considered an indicator of the extent not only of their appreciation of gender equality principles but also of the relevance of the GMS GSIP activities and outputs to the needs and aspirations of the GMS countries and the GMS regional cooperation program.

---

[49] This estimated cost and financing is a tentative estimate and may be subject to change as the GMS GSIP is operationalized.

Equal opportunity for women. Zhengli is the deputy director of the Lijiang Railway Station in Yunnan Province. While GMS countries have made progress toward gender equality, the GMS Gender Strategy found that gender inequalities remained and were compounded by other social categorizations, such as disability, age, rural or urban location, and sexual orientation.

APPENDIX 1:
Greater Mekong Subregion Program Institutional Structure and the Roles of its Different Levels in Implementing the Greater Mekong Subregion Program Gender Strategy

GMS Program Institutional Structure	Role in the GMS Gender Strategy Implementation Plan (for confirmation)
1. GMS Summit • The highest forum in the GMS Economic Cooperation Program • Follows the standard structure for a leaders' summit, with plenary meetings and an informal leaders' retreat • Organized once every 3 years in a GMS country to (i) provide broad strategic directions for future actions under the GMS Economic Cooperation Program, (ii) endorse GMS strategic frameworks and related investment plans, and (iii) endorse other GMS policies and strategies	Will review the GMS Gender Strategy Implementation Plan for notation at the 8th GMS Leaders' Summit in 2024
2. GMS Ministerial Conference • Organized annually • Represents cooperation at the policy and strategic levels • Serves as the venue in which member governments interact and coordinate with development partners, including the private sector	Review the progress of the GMS Program including implementation of the GMS Gender Strategy Implementation Plan
3. GMS Senior Officials' Meeting • Overall coordination mechanisms under the GMS Program, encompassing both the policy and organizational aspects of program cooperation • Composed of GMS national coordinators, who are also heads of the GMS National Secretariat of the individual GMS countries • Although the Ministerial Conference is the main strategy- and policy-setting body in the GMS Program, the SOM is where proposals are initially formulated and operational plans and programs emanating from the various sector-level working groups and forums are reviewed and vetted.	Review and/or endorse the following: 1. GMS Gender Strategy Implementation Plan 2. Revised gender indicators of the GMS-2030 Results Framework

GMS Program Institutional Structure	Role in the GMS Gender Strategy Implementation Plan (for confirmation)

4. GMS Sector Working Groups and Forums
• Key operational apparatus of the GMS Program
  • Formulate their sector strategic frameworks, action plans, and budget
  • Provides operational leadership and technical guidance to plan, implement, monitor, and evaluate subregional sector activities
  • Monitor strategic program and project results
  • Prepare progress reports for submission to the GMS sector ministers and GMS national secretariats
	1. Update their respective sectors' strategic frameworks and action plans to align with the GMS Gender Strategy (may be done with the assistance of a gender specialist)
	2. Enhance their sector's gender equality performance indicators in the GMS-2030 Results Framework
	3. Review the design of RIF projects under their respective sectors and propose gender features to be included in the project design
	4. Review the project completion reports under their respective sectors to assess the relevance and substance of the projects' gender equality results
	5. Review the design of lateral learning workshops and attend these workshops
	6. Review the design of Gender Forums and attend these forums
	7. Review the design of the gender diagnostic of their respective sectors and assist in conducting the diagnostic
	8. Review and validate the guidelines or tip sheet on mainstreaming gender in their respective sectors (to be drafted by a gender specialist for each sector)

5. GMS National Secretariats • Ensures smooth and effective coordination at the country level	Assist the GMS Task Force on Gender in assessing the contributions of the GMS Program Gender Strategy's implementation to the country's delivery of their commitments to gender equality promotion

GMS Program Institutional Structure	Role in the GMS Gender Strategy Implementation Plan (for confirmation)
6. GMS Task Force on Gender • To be formed to supervise the implementation of this plan and monitor the achievement of the objectives of the Gender Strategy	1. Lead the enhancement and clarification of the gender performance indicators of the GMS-2030 Results Framework; and assess if there is a need to develop a stand-alone regional gender results framework (separate from the GMS-2030 Results Framework) 2. Ensure that the Gender Strategy Implementation Plan activities, outputs, and outcomes, including those of the eight sectors, support the national gender frameworks and policies of the GMS countries and the gender equality aspirations of the GMS program. 3. Guide the eight sectors in developing the gender equality aspects of their respective sector strategic frameworks and action plans 4. Develop guidelines for mainstreaming gender in the design of RIF projects for presentation to the development partners and endorsement of the GMS senior officials and ministers 5. Guide the GMS secretariat in preparing the GMS projects' gender database (including which projects have effectively mainstreamed gender in their design and projects that achieved their gender equality targets at completion) 6. Lead the preparation of the design of the gender forums and moderate them
7. GMS Secretariat • Based in the Regional Cooperation and Operations Coordination Division of ADB Southeast Asia Department • Provide administrative and technical support to the GMS Task Force on Gender, GMS national secretariats, GMS sector working groups, and GMS senior officials	1. Generate/mobilize funds (e.g., seek financial support from development partners) for the delivery of the Gender Strategy Implementation Plan 2. Assist the Task Force on Gender in supervising the implementation and monitoring of the achievements and gaps of the Gender Strategy Implementation Plan

ADB = Asian Development Bank, GMS = Greater Mekong Subregion, RIF = Regional Investment Framework, SOM = Senior Officials' Meeting.

Notes:
• The description of the different levels of the GMS Program's institutional structure is from the GMS Secretariat, Asian Development Bank. 2016. *Study on Strengthening the Greater Mekong Subregion Program's Institutional Framework.*
• The roles of the different levels of the GMS institutional structure in implementing the GMS Gender Strategy are for validation of the GMS Secretariat, GMS national secretariats, GMS sector working groups and Forums, and GMS senior officials.

Source: GMS Secretariat.

APPENDIX 2:
Greater Mekong Subregion Gender Strategy's Crosscutting Themes and Examples of Actions Per Theme

Theme	Actions
1. Macroeconomic coordination	• Support gender-responsive budgeting • Analyze the distributional economic impacts of projects at the regional level • Analyze national policies to identify areas for reform and program support to promote equal economic opportunities for women and other groups
2. Labor mobility and safe migration	• Promote gender-responsive safe internal mobility and lifelong skills, especially for female migrants from minority ethnic groups and gender-diverse individuals who are vulnerable to exploitation and harassment • Provide education and training on migrants' opportunities and rights in conjunction with GMS countries and international NGOs
3. Education and skills	• Pursue the inclusion of formal technical and vocational education and training and leadership education for women and girls in nontraditional roles and sectors (such as public and the public sector, STEM education areas, defense, and national security) • Include gender targets in employment and training in infrastructure investments with employment opportunities • Promote links to local education institutions and partnerships (e.g., scholarships, paid internships, mentoring, and flexible work arrangements, such as part-time work and work-from-home)
4. Special economic zones	• Support investment in equal employment opportunities at all levels in special economic zones through incorporating core labor standards and gender-responsive human resource policies (e.g., childcare, access to health care)
5. Digitalization and new technologies	• Enhance partnerships with the private sector, NGOs, and financiers to facilitate access and connection to the use of digital technology by marginalized groups through financing and training programs • Identify opportunities to support women in technical and leadership roles in digital technology and e-commerce and provide pathways for them to enter ICT fields directly from education or existing employment
6. Gender norms and attitudes	• Promote inclusion and change attitudes to gender norms that favor one group over another • Promote inclusive language in public communications • Conduct gender analysis informed by an intersectional lens across GMS region programs as an important step toward a sustainable and gender-equal GMS region

GMS = Greater Mekong Subregion; ICT = information and communication technology; NGO = nongovernment organization; STEM = science, technology, engineering, and mathematics.

Source: ADB. 2022. *Greater Mekong Subregion Gender Strategy*. pp. 7–8.

APPENDIX 3:
Greater Mekong Subregion Gender Strategy Implementation Plan Gantt Chart of Activities

Activities by GMS Gender Strategy Objectives	2025				2026				2027				2028				2029				2030			
	Q1	Q2	Q3	Q4	Q1	Q2	Q3	Q4	Q1	Q2	Q3	Q4	Q1	Q2	Q3	Q4	Q1	Q2	Q3	Q4	Q1	Q2	Q3	Q4
GENERAL (for all three objectives). Management Systems for Delivering the GMS Gender Strategy Implementation Plan																								
1. Form a GMS task force on gender as a mechanism for implementing and monitoring the progress of the delivery of activities to achieve each objective of the GMS Strategy and for disseminating lessons learned	✗																							
2. Conduct a review of the GMS Gender Strategy Implementation Plan (and achievements) at midterm and completion												✗											✗	
Objective 1. Improve existing methods and develop new and innovative approaches to gender mainstreaming to ensure equal access and participation in opportunities arising from the GMS Program																								
3. Assess in-depth the eight GMS sectors' existing methods for gender mainstreaming		✗		✗																				
4. Improve the gender equality features of the eight sectors' strategic frameworks and action plans in line with GMS countries' aspirations.				✗	✗																			
5. Design and conduct subregional lateral learning workshops on mainstreaming gender in pillar 1 (community) and pillar 2 (connectivity) sectors every 3 years						✗[a]												✗						
6. Design and conduct subregional lateral learning workshops on mainstreaming gender equality in pillar 3 (competitiveness) sectors every 3 years						✗[a]													✗					
7. Develop a guidance note for designing the gender features and assessing the gender equality results of RIF projects in consultation with GMS stakeholders (including development partners)			✗																					
8. Enhance the gender equality performance indicators at Levels 1, 2, and 3 of the GMS Strategy 2030 results framework									✗															
Objective 2. Complement subregional efforts to explicitly address gender barriers affecting the full participation of individuals of all ages, abilities, and in all socioeconomic spheres																								
9. Conduct a study on the gender barriers experienced by individuals of all ages, abilities (and disabilities) in all socioeconomic spheres, and initiatives (good practices) in the subregion to address these barriers																	✗	✗						
10. Develop case studies on the GMS Program's good practices and accomplishments in gender mainstreaming																			✗	✗	✗			
11. Conduct a multi-stakeholder forum on subregional efforts to respond to the intersection of gender inequality with old age, disabilities, ethnicity, educational and income levels, and geographic location																						✗		
Objective 3. Address pervasive gender norms that disadvantage one group over another																								
12. Conduct gender forums on any or all of the GMS Gender Strategy crosscutting themes every 3 years (the selection of topics will be based on the demand of GMS countries and sectors)						✗[a]												✗						
13. Pilot a project for women's employment (jobs and entrepreneurship) and leadership in a nontraditional sector (e.g., energy or transport) at the GMS level (time includes the preparation and processing of a TA proposal for this project).						✗[a]	✗	✗	✗	✗	✗	✗	✗	✗	✗	✗	✗	✗	✗	✗	✗	✗	✗	✗

GMS = Greater Mekong Subregion, Q = quarter, RIF = Regional Investment Framework, TA = technical assistance.
[a] To cut costs, the first two lateral learning workshops will be held back-to-back with the first Gender Forum in the second quarter of 2025, and the second two lateral learning workshops will be held back-to-back with the second Gender Forum in the second quarter of 2029.
Source: GMS Secretariat.

APPENDIX 4:
Assessment of the Gender Elements of the Greater Mekong Subregion Sectors' Strategic Frameworks

AGRICULTURE

The Core Agriculture Support Program's Strategy for Promoting Safe and Environment-friendly Agro-based Value Chains in the Greater Mekong Subregion (GMS) and Siem Reap Action Plan, 2018–2022 (SASRAP) has no gender analysis of the agriculture sector in the subregion. However, gender equality is explicit in the overall purpose ("security of safe food for all, irrespective of a person's demographic, income status, and gender"), common guiding principles ("gender empowerment"), and design and monitoring framework (with gender-related performance indicators at the outcome level and two of four outputs).[1] To apply the "gender empowerment" principle, the SASRAP states,

"Policy development should address activities that will empower women and ensure equal benefit sharing between women and men. There is potential for empowering women and men smallholder farmers by introducing gender-sensitive agronomic practices that can strengthen their capacity in production, processing, and trade as well as improve gender equity in [the] agriculture sector with equal opportunity and benefit sharing for women and men." The design and monitoring framework for the SASRAP has gender performance indicators at the outcome level and two of four outputs.

ENVIRONMENTAL SUSTAINABILITY AND CLIMATE CHANGE

The GMS Core Environment Program Strategic Framework and Action Plan 2018–2022 assesses the challenges faced in implementing the Core Environment Plan Phase II, including inadequate resources for and isolation of its gender and social inclusion elements, and the need to include social and gender-disaggregated indicators in the design and monitoring framework.[2] This is a partial gender assessment, as it does not cover access to environmental resources and governance in the subregion. However, its guiding principles for adopting an integrated value-chain approach include promoting gender and social inclusiveness. Nonetheless, the Core

Dali-Lijiang Railway Project. A woman from the Xiaoshui Meishang Village has worked in the station since 2011, cooking for 15 railway employees and sanitizing the railway station, providing her a fair monthly income.

---

[1]   Asian Development Bank (ADB). 2018. *Strategy for Promoting Safe and Environment-Friendly Agro-based Value Chains in the GMS and Siem Reap Action Plan, 2018–2022.* pp. viii, 15, and 39–43.

[2]   GMS Environment Operations Center, ADB. 2017. *Greater Mekong Subregion Core Environment Program Strategic Framework and Action Plan 2018–2022.*

Environment Plan does not explicitly promote gender equality in its strategic approach, thematic areas, types of service intervention, and activities. Its only other gender feature is in its indirect benefits to households ("gender-inclusive employment opportunities from more integrated value chains") and communities ("greater social and gender inclusion").[3]

HEALTH COOPERATION

The GMS Health Cooperation Strategy 2019–2023 has a partial sector gender analysis because while its appendix provides sex-disaggregated data on the population and key health indicators in the six countries, its main text lacks explicit mention of the need to understand and respond to the distinct health needs and health-seeking behavior of women and men in the subregion. Moreover, while it mentions linguistic, cultural, and financial barriers as limiting access to essential health services and socioeconomic inequalities as increasing vulnerability to disease, a gender analysis of these barriers and inequalities is not explicit.[4] However, the advancement of gender equality is in its statement of principles and objectives, including gender mainstreaming as one of the crosscutting themes of its programmatic areas. Its description of gender mainstreaming as a crosscutting theme mentions support measures (e.g., regional action plans will actively address participation by and for women and gender perspectives will be integrated into all research and knowledge products). Its strategic results framework (in a separate document) has key gender indicators in three key performance areas:[5]

(i) **Key Performance Indicator 2.3.1. Health Impact Assessment of GMS Urban and Transport Infrastructure Development:** Working Group on Health Cooperation (WGHC) policy advocacy and technical support are implemented to wider adoption of health impact assessments, environmental impact assessments, or environmental health impact assessments for new Regional Investment Framework projects of the GMS Urban and Transport sectors, located in special economic zones and focused on road safety. The key assumption for this key performance indicator is that using these tools by the non-health sector will mitigate any negative health impacts affecting vulnerable populations, especially women, children, and ethnic minorities, from projects that facilitate regional integration.

(ii) **Key Performance Indicator 3.1.2. Regional Health Cooperation Leadership.** GMS countries have incorporated relevant crosscutting themes (e.g., in-country policy convergence, gender mainstreaming, and inclusive and equitable development) and enablers in the design of new WGHC-initiated Regional Investment Framework projects and WGHC annual workplan activities.

(iii) **Key Performance Indicator 3.2.1. Intra-regional Capacity Building.** Sex-disaggregated number of public health personnel who participated (as trainer and trainee) in WGHC-defined intra-regional capacity building activities, learning exchanges, and information sharing among GMS countries on health (e.g., medicine, nursing, public health, field epidemiology, traditional and indigenous medicines, health research, etc.) between 2019 to 2023.

---

[3]   Footnote 2, p. 33.
[4]   ADB. 2019. *Greater Mekong Subregion Health Cooperation Strategy 2019–2023.* p. 4.
[5]   ADB. 2020. *Strategic Results Framework for the Greater Mekong Subregion Health Cooperation Strategy 2019–2023.*

TOURISM

Promoting gender equality first appeared in the GMS Tourism Sector Strategy 2006–2015, which aimed to, among others "contribute to poverty reduction, gender equality, empowerment of women, and sustainable development." While this objective is not explicit in the succeeding GMS Tourism Sector Strategy 2016–2025, gender equality has remained one of its crosscutting themes.[6] The gender analysis in this succeeding sector strategy is considered as partial as the analysis focused solely on the employment opportunities provided by the tourism industry and not on the gendered needs of women and men tourists and making the tourism infrastructures and services responsive to these distinct needs. Gender mainstreaming in approaches and implementation structures is also partial because although gender equality is explicitly mentioned among its crosscutting themes ("Tourism and tourism-related policies, programs, and projects will be formulated and implemented based on sound gender analysis. Women and men will have equal rights and equal access to resources, economic opportunities, education, training, and decision making"); the translation of this crosscutting theme into specific approaches is not clear. The gender equality elements are not explicit in the sector's strategic directions, programs, and results framework.

URBAN DEVELOPMENT

The GMS Urban Development Strategic Framework 2015–2022 assessed the "possibility that certain groups of society do not benefit equally with other groups. These disadvantaged or vulnerable segments include the poor, women and children, smaller ethnic groups, migrant workers, students, and the disabled."[7] It also acknowledges women and migrant workers as tending "to feature

Women in tourism projects. A woman from Son Trach commune, in Quang Binh province, Viet Nam, transports tourists in her boat as part of the Asian Development Bank GMS Sustainable Tourism Development Project.

---

[6]   Mekong Tourism Coordinating Office. 2017. *Greater Mekong Subregion Tourism Sector Strategy 2016–2025.*
[7]   ADB. 2015. *Greater Mekong Subregion Urban Development Strategic Framework 2015–2022.*

prominently among cross-border migrant workers in both the formal and informal sectors."[8] With this explicit recognition of this social problem, the strategic framework is assessed to have a gender analysis. However, the analysis is partial because it lacks in-depth discussion of gender issues in urban development. With regard to gender equality principles, one of the crosscutting themes of the Strategic Framework is "inclusive development," which the framework explains as providing measures to identify potentially vulnerable groups, including women, and ensure that they benefit from the framework's initiatives." Given this, the framework has substantial gender equality principles and objectives. However, gender elements are not explicit in its action plans (e.g., description of the capacity development programs and development of a data resource) and results framework.

ENERGY AND TRANSPORT

The reviewed energy[9] and transport[10] sector strategies do not mention any gender elements. In the transport sector strategic framework, the assessed risk of increased trafficking of women and children due to improved mobility and accessibility is considered in this assessment as a social safeguards concern rather than a gender issue.

---

8 Footnote 7, p. 13.
9 ADB. 2016. *Greater Mekong Subregion Energy Sector Assessment, Strategy, and Roadmap*.
10 ADB. 2018. *GMS Transport Sector Strategy 2030: Toward a Seamless, Efficient, Reliable, and Sustainable GMS Transport System*.